IT HAPPENED IN NEW ORLEANS

It Happened In Series

IT HAPPENED IN NEW ORLEANS

Bonnye E. Stuart

TWODOT®

GUILFORD, CONNECTICUT
HELENA, MONTANA
AN IMPRINT OF THE GLOBE PEQUOT PRESS

A · TWODOT® · BOOK

Text design by Nancy Freeborn
Map by M. A. Dubé © 2007 Morris Book Publishing, LLC
Front cover photo: LePetre, House of the Turk, Dauphiné Street, New Orleans. Library of Congress, LC-DIG-ppmsca-09508
Back cover photo: William McKinley making a speech from a balcony in New Orleans. Library of Congress, LC-USZ62-98368

Library of Congress Cataloging-in-Publication Data
Stuart, Bonnye.
It happened in New Orleans / Bonnye Stuart.—1st ed.
p. cm.—(It happened in series)
Includes bibliographical references and index.
ISBN-13: 978-0-7627-3905-9
ISBN-10: 0-7627-3905-3
1. New Orleans (La.)—History—Anecdotes. 2. New Orleans (La.)—Biography—Anecdotes. I. Title.
F379.N545S88 2006
976.3'35—dc22

2006025487

Manufactured in the United States of America
First Edition/First Printing

CONTENTS

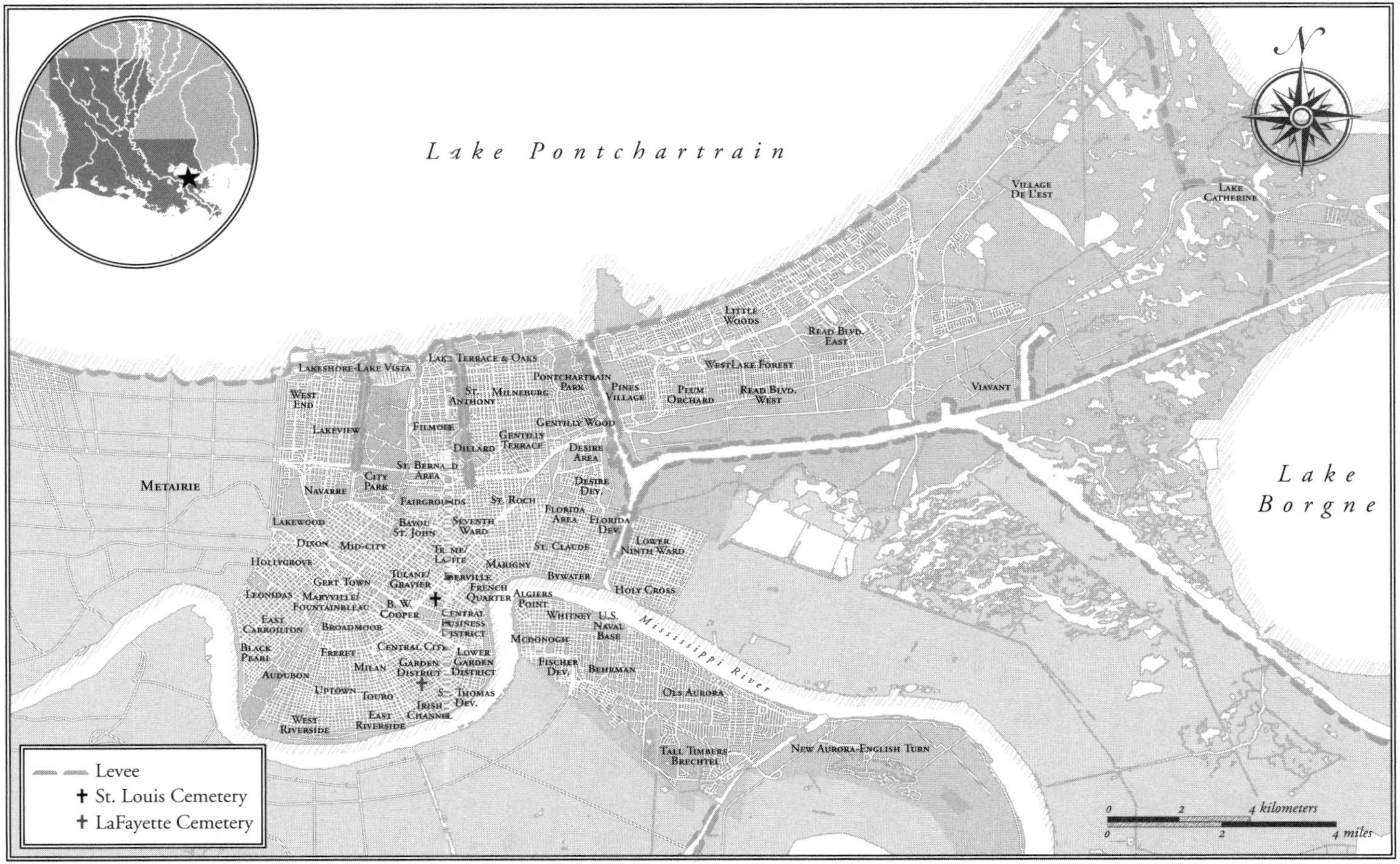

N
Lake Pontchartrain
Lake Borgne
Village De L'Est
Lake Catherine
Little Woods
Read Blvd. East
WestLake Forest
Plum Orchard
Read Blvd. West
Viavant
Pines Village
Pontchartrain Park
Lake Terrace & Oaks
Lakeshore-Lake Vista
West End
St. Anthony
Milneburg
Gentilly Wood
Gentilly Terrace
Lakeview
Filmore
Dillard
Desire Area
Desire Dev.
St. Bernard Area
City Park
Metairie
Navarre
Fairgrounds
St. Roch
Florida Area
Florida Dev.
Lakewood
Bayou St. John
Seventh Ward
St. Claude
Lower Ninth Ward
Dixon
Mid-City
Marigny
Hollygrove
Bywater
Gert Town
Tulane/Gravier
Holy Cross
French Quarter
Leonidas
Maryville/Fountainbleau
B. W. Cooper
Algiers Point
Whitney
U.S. Naval Base
East Carrollton
Broadmoor
Central Business District
Mississippi River
McDonogh
Black Pearl
Freret
Central City
Lower Garden District
Milan
Garden District
Fischer Dev.
Behrman
Audubon
Uptown
Touro
St. Thomas Dev.
Ols Aurora
West Riverside
East Riverside
Irish Channel
Tall Timbers-Brechtel
New Aurora-English Turn
Levee
St. Louis Cemetery
LaFayette Cemetery
0 2 4 kilometers
0 2 4 miles

NEW ORLEANS

ACKNOWLEDGMENTS

I am a ninth-generation New Orleanian, dating back to Jean Baptiste Perret, a Dauphiné merchant who arrived in the city in 1723 from Grenoble, France. My ancestors were part of the city's early history and lived and worked through many of the events I researched for this collection of stories. Though no one in my family was very famous or infamous, it was intriguing to think about how the Perrets figured in the city's past. What did Charles and Joseph lose when the city burned in 1788? How did Paul and Jeanne survive the yellow fever epidemics? Where were Louis and Adelaide when the Union forces captured the city? Did any of my great-great-uncles play chess with Paul Morphy or catch a glimpse of Degas roaming the streets? Did any ancestral cousins or aunts yell with excitement at the Great State Post Stake race?

As tenth-generation New Orleanians, my children are are part of my city's future. I have tried to imagine what events they will endure, what their stories will be, and who will chronicle them.

I would like to thank all my ancestors for surviving and thriving in this place I call home, so that in 2006 I would be able to record a few chosen memories of our wondrous city.

New Orleanians are still surviving. Katrina, the villain of the last chapter, is very vivid in the minds of all of us who love New Orleans. A favorite uncle died just after the hurricane, and my younger cousin had a fatal heart attack while evacuating. Neither was in the official death count. One cousin and her family were rescued from their roof; aunts and uncles lost their homes; friends must rebuild not only houses but entire lives; my sister lost everything and relocated to Baton Rouge; my son's job moved to a city miles away. But the family survives.

Thanks go to all those who contributed to my research. Paul Kirchner gave me material on dueling, and Farron L. Kempton helped out with information on the Great State Post Stake race. Much gratitude goes to those who developed the Internet and the remarkable search engines. I was able to do much of my research on the Web, searching archives and various collections, magazines, newspapers, and official New Orleans Web sites. Winthrop University, where I teach in the Mass and Speech Communication Departments, and my colleague, Marilyn Sarow, provided the intellectual stimulation needed to stay the course on this long journey. Thanks to Megan Hiller for all her help and confidence in my ability to get the job done. Much appreciation also goes to sister-in-law Gloria Butcher, cousin Pam Perret, and sisters Daphne and Gina, who sent me material on various New Orleans happenings and always encouraged me to write a "good" story. They keep me connected to all areas of the city.

Thanks for their constant reassurance go to my four children, David, Elizabeth, Jessica, and Christian; sons-in-law, Frank and Jeff; daughter-in-law, Jessica Lee, and daughter-in-law-to-be, Ruby. Big hugs for their inspiring spirit of youth go to granddaughters, Emily, Lauren, and Tennyson, and grandsons, Jack and Braden. Much love and gratefulness go to my loving and loved husband, Laurence, the true raconteur of our family. I also have to thank him for my new computer on which I will finish this manuscript.

Learning more about my beloved city by researching and recording her unique and compelling stories has been a great joy for me, and my hope is that you, too, can experience the ultimate joy of telling your own stories.

INTRODUCTION

New Orleans was founded on a small bit of marshy land hugged tightly by the imposing Mississippi River. Her potential to rule the country's largest river and provide a vital outlet for trade and commerce could not be ignored. The French, Spanish, and English all tried to call New Orleans theirs for a while, but it was the Americans who eventually came away with the prize. They flooded into New Orleans as traders, settlers, businessmen, bankers, sports enthusiasts, musicians, and artists. German, Italian, and Irish families chose to settle in the city; slaves from Africa and the islands, impressed sailors, convicts, and military men came forcibly. Religious zealots, fishermen, fortune seekers, trappers, voodoo queens, farmers, and high-society men and women all lived and worked side by side in the shadow of the Father of Waters. Native Americans, Islanders, Creoles, and Cajuns contributed their cultural characteristics to the unique mix of peoples, creating one of the most exotic cities in the New World.

By the time New Orleans became an American city in 1803, she had already lived multiple lives; many of her citizens spoke French and Spanish as easily as English. She was never without a "story to tell" and there are many still waiting to be written. This book features just a few of the interesting and entertaining tales of a city and her inhabitants.

Today New Orleans continues to attract adventurers, artists, rabble-rousers, storytellers, entrepreneurs, daredevils, rogues, wanderers, and others drawn by the irresistible excitement of "The City that Care Forgot." From January to December, New Orleans fills with wonder and revelry. Mardi Gras, St. Joseph's Day parades, the Tennessee Williams Literary Festival, the Crescent City Classic 10K, the Jazz and Heritage Festival, and the Celebration in the Oaks are just a few of her annual festivities. Residents and tourists alike enjoy riding historic streetcars up St. Charles Avenue or taking sweaty swamp tours to search for alligators, dining at Galatoire's or grabbing a po-boy in a little hole in the wall along Bourbon Street, visiting a museum or a casino, listening to jazz or the Blues, indulging in a powdered beignet or taking a trip to the French Market for a huge bag of shelled pecans. All of this is New Orleans.

So sit back and take a ride through the mysterious and enchanted past of old New Orleans. Kick off your shoes, grab a cup of coffee, with chicory, of course, and feel free to laugh and cry with the odd characters who spice up local stories of devastation, wonder, and craziness. You are soon to be part of the story that is New Orleans.

PLAYING A TRICK ON THE ENGLISH

- 1699 -

THE "ISLAND," AS THE FRENCH DESCRIBED IT, would eventually become the city of New Orleans, though it was not a tropical paradise. Surrounded by the muddy waters of the Mississippi and various lakes and bayous, the Delta was a damp, mosquito-infested swamp. Yet many countries were trying to gain a foothold in the murky wetlands. What they ultimately wanted was control of the mighty river itself.

The Spanish, who had branched out from their colonies in Florida, and the English, not satisfied with the Atlantic Coast, were both looking for a route up the Mississippi River. The French had explored the lower Mississippi Valley, but even they had not found a navigable route from the Gulf of Mexico north to solid ground. By the close of the seventeenth century, however, one country would finally make claims on the lower Mississippi; this coup would not be achieved by might or power, but by cunning.

It had been seventeen years since La Salle had laid claim to the basin of the Mississippi for France. He had traveled the lower area where the salty gulf water met the fresh river water, yet no route had been found up the river. La Salle had tried but had ended up on the coast of Texas, hundreds of miles away. Iberville and Bienville, sons of a Canadian fur trader, began their search. The brothers were determined to be the first to find and take control of Mississippi River trade routes.

On his first expedition Iberville found an entrance to the river, and needing to garner support for further exploration, he departed almost immediately for France. Younger brother Bienville, a fierce commander and seven-year veteran of his brother's frontier warfare, was left in charge of meeting with the native tribes in the area and eliciting their help to find routes connecting the gulf to the river. Iberville had written that the area was hard to navigate, "low and flooded, covered with reeds as thick as one's finger and 10 to 15 feet tall." He also talked about an endless supply of blackberries and a "great quantity of wild game, such as ducks, geese, snipe, teal, bustards, and other birds." The Frenchmen, based out of a Biloxi outpost on the gulf, were eager to establish a trading post on the great river.

On the morning of September 15, 1699, Bienville, with his new title of king's lieutenant in hand, and five of his men set off from Biloxi in two canoes. They explored westward, paddling through Pass Manchac into the river. Knowing they had found a viable passage through to the gulf, they scooted south, slipping easily around the sharp natural bends in the river. All went well for a while, until they rounded a sharp bend. Trouble lay just ahead.

Anchored in the shallow water along the bank was an ominous English warship, the *Carolina Galley*. The English, too, had penetrated the maze of swamps and waterways of the river's delta and found a route northward from the gulf to the land upriver. The ship had sailed from London almost a year earlier to survey the northern coast of the Gulf of Mexico in search of a settlement site for the Carolina Company.

The two opposing forces now met each other, an English commander with a dangerous warship heading north and the five Frenchmen with two bark canoes heading south.

About 70 miles above the mouth of the river, the English ship was careened in a bend in the river 3 leagues long, and its stationary position gave Bienville time to assess the situation quickly. The British twelve-gun corvette was a formidable foe, certainly one Bienville's two canoes and few men could not take on. He knew they could never overpower the ship, but Bienville also realized that to turn away now and allow the British ship to continue north up the river could mean giving up France's claim to the lower part of the Mississippi. He was determined not to do that.

Bienville waved to the warship. His yells were answered by commander Captain Lewis Banks, a navy man of some renown. Bienville boarded the English ship and accused the captain of intruding on French territory. Banks had a haughty attitude sustained by the warship's power beneath his feet. He spoke of challenging France's claims to the river land and outlined his intentions to proceed north as soon as favorable winds were available. He reported that he had fended off Indian attacks to get this far and would proceed as soon as the weather allowed. He had colonists aboard the *Carolina Galley,* French Huguenots who would be establishing a settlement to be called Carolana on the Mississippi River as soon as they reached solid land. Britain was famous for taking extreme measures to establish an area—intense exploration, immigration, military might, and trade negotiations.

Bienville was incensed. France had claim to that land and was already working to establish an outpost upriver. Banks's audacity was no match for Bienville's bravado. Bienville thought fast and then deviously explained to Banks that he and his men were just an expeditionary force and that the rest of the French fleet was around the next bend. Bienville told Banks he was trespassing on French territory. Bienville added he would not hesitate to use force to get Banks to vacate his position. Banks was aware of the French fleet's reputation.

Still Banks hesitated.

Bienville threatened that the French fleet would soon be in sight, adding that his brother Iberville was in command. Banks was now worried. Just three years earlier, Iberville's forty-four-gun *Pelican* had defeated three English warships with a total of 124 guns. Banks had actually been captured and taken prisoner by Iberville. He now recognized Bienville as the brother of his victor. Being defeated by this pair of ruthless Frenchmen was not a situation he wanted to repeat.

Bienville, now fully committed to this guise, turned his head and feigned a signal to his fleet for support. He then ordered Banks out of France's territory. The parlay between the adversaries was over.

Banks fell for Bienville's bluff. He feared his twelve guns would be no match for the heavily armed French fleet just upstream. He hoisted anchor, turned his ship around, and sailed south, down the Mississippi River. Cursing the Frenchman, he retreated but promised to return with greater force to settle the Mississippi River another time.

When Bienville reported back to his brother about the skirmish, he is reported to have modestly stated, "I obliged the English to abandon their enterprise."

Iberville remembered the captain as "a scatterbrain full of English presumption and of little ability" and gave no credence to the Englishman's parting threat to return.

When mapmakers in France heard of the incident, they named the now famous bend in the river *Detour a l'Anglais,* or *English Turn,* to commemorate the spot where the English fled, leaving the Mississippi and all her surrounding lands to the French monarch. English Turn is remembered for the protection it afforded the yet-to-be-established French city of New Orleans. If it had not been for what occurred at English Turn, New Orleans would never have been established. The English Turn trickery marked the beginning of French domination in the Mississippi Valley area from 1699 to 1763.

Captain Banks has given historians some concern, being called Banks, Bank, Bond, and Barr in various historical sources, but he is nonetheless the captain of the *Carolina Galley* that turned around because of Bienville's ruse. Jean Baptiste Le Moyne, Sieur de Bienville, went on to found the city of New Orleans, and today English Turn, just fifteen minutes from downtown New Orleans, is famous for its Jack Nicklaus golf and country-club community.

LIGHTING A CANDLE AND SAYING A PRAYER

- 1788 -

Don Jose Vicente Nunez had lived in New Orleans for nearly twenty years as army paymaster and military treasurer of the colony after the French ceded the Louisiana Territory to Spain. He had done well and had moved into a large townhouse built in 1783 at 619 Chartres Street.

The Lenten season was almost over for devotees in the predominantly Catholic city. It was March 21, 1788, Good Friday, the day of atonement and mourning, the observance of the crucifixion of Jesus Christ. Tomorrow would be Holy Saturday, and then Easter Sunday would dawn gloriously as the most sacred day in the Catholic faith, greater even than Christmas.

Like many other devout Catholics, Nunez had set up a small chapel in his home. Here he would pray to God and light candles in remembrance of holy days. Following the prescribed ritual of Good Friday, he ceremoniously lit his altar candles.

New Orleans, normally a loud and vibrant city, was quiet during this penitent time. All celebrations, parties, and galas were banned. It was a day of hushed prayer. But Mother Nature was not to be tamed. The early spring day was blustery. Gale force winds blew in from the south and swirled through French Quarter galleries and into the open homes.

An old beggar passing the corner of Toulouse and Chartres Streets noticed flames pouring out of a second story window. He cried out, loud and clear, "Fire!" Nunez heard the man yelling and realized his home was ablaze. The lit candles had set the lace window curtains on fire.

The city had an alarm system for emergencies such as this. The bells of the Church of St. Louis would ring out across the quarter to alert the citizenry. But this day the bells would not sound. It was a holy day of mourning for Catholics, and the bells never tolled on Good Friday. They remained silent.

The only alarm would be the beggar's urgent cry.

The fire was out of control from the start. The city was ill-equipped to handle such catastrophes, and although there were two municipal fire engines, they could not be used. They were engulfed in flames themselves. Sparks leaped from building to building, from homes to offices, leaving only destruction behind in the Plaza de Armas, the now Spanish French Quarter. The fire was fanned by the relentless wind. People spilled out into the streets. Mothers huddled around their children while the men tried to save their belongings.

When the fire was over, the damage was extensive. More than 800 homes and many public buildings lay in ashes. The devastation stretched from Chartres to Dauphiné Streets and from Conti to St. Philip. More than half the city lay in scorched ruins, and many citizens had little or no possessions left and nowhere to live.

Father Antonio de Sedella, called Pere Antoine, pastor of the Church of St. Louis (it would not become the historic St. Louis Cathedral for six more years), was heartbroken to see the charred ruins of his church. The town hall and the presbytere or priests' house were also gone. The conflagration consumed the parish archives and took down the *cabildo,* an old-world colombage structure of brick and wood. The prison was burned to the ground, but the prisoners had been miraculously rescued in a mad scramble to free them from their cells.

The Ursuline nuns, fearful that their convent would also fall to the fire's wrath, prayed fervently to Notre Dame de Bon Secours, Our Lady of Prompt Succor, patron of Rouen, the French city where they had come from, that the flames would not overtake the convent. Their entreaties were answered. The Ursuline convent on Chartres Street was spared.

A correspondent for the *Gazette des Deux-Ponts,* a French international newspaper read in London, Versailles, Berlin, Rome, and Vienna, was visiting New Orleans and reported on the sickening scene of vast destruction. He wrote: "In order to appreciate the horror of the conflagration, it suffices to say that in less than five hours more than eight hundred and sixteen buildings were reduced to ashes. . . . in the place of the flourishing city of the day before, nothing but rubbish and heaps of ruins, pale and trembling mothers, dragging their children along by the hand, their despair not even leaving them the strength to weep or groan."

Governor Esteban Miro rose to the task of caring for the displaced citizens of the city. He set up tents for the homeless and supplied victims with food and other provisions. Miro wrote to the Spanish authorities for money and aid, describing in detail the "abject misery, crying and sobbing" of the city's citizenry as proof of the total devastation.

There was reason to be thankful, however. Not a single person died in the fire. Many said it was due in part to the urgent cries of the beggar who first noticed the fire in the window of Nunez's house. Others said it was God's will. The *Gazette des Deux-Ponts* verified this remarkable statistic, reporting that "not a man perished."

In the wake of the fire, an angel emerged. Don Andes Almonaster y Roxas had made his fortune in the city. He had been married, at the age of sixty, to Creole Louise de Laronde in the Church of St. Louis in 1787, a year before the fire. He committed his monetary resources to rebuilding the church and its surrounding buildings, finer than they had been before. Many others in the city began reconstructing their homes and offices. The Spanish government sent money for the construction of "huts" for the homeless. But New Orleans would never again be the quaint French village it had been prior to the Great Fire of 1788.

Spanish architecture would dictate the new construction. Thick stucco rather than the prevailing wooden materials would be used. The old French peaked roofs of ax-hewn cypress shingles would be replaced with flat Spanish baked tiled roofs. The Spaniards built a new *cabildo* to replace the smaller town hall. The impressive stucco structure, now called the Cabildo, dominated the plaza and served as a testament to Spanish rule in New Orleans.

The city struggled to rebuild itself. Money was hard to come by and materials were in short supply. It was a year before the burned out remains of the Church of St. Louis were removed and construction of a new church begun. Scarcely had the city recovered when a second terrible fire broke out in 1794 and burned another 200 buildings.

Again the Spanish throne was called upon for monies to rebuild the colony and aid its citizens. It made the necessary investment, but Spain wouldn't call the city its own for long. Nine years later, in 1803, New Orleans would be turned over to the Americans.

In 1988, exactly 200 years after the Great Fire of 1788, the Cabildo was partially destroyed by fire. It has since been carefully restored. Some of the few buildings still standing today that escaped the devastating fires of 1788 and 1794 are Lafitte's blacksmith shop, the Custom House, and Charity Hospital.

SINGING INTO HISTORY

- 1796 -

Now in the final decade of Spanish rule, New Orleans was becoming a bustling city. Small, shabby houses stretched back five or six blocks deep for about a mile along the Mississippi River, the main thoroughfare for business and pleasure. Visitors traveling to the city by land had to make sure to arrive before the city gates were closed at 9:00 P.M. Any person departing the city was required to post a representative bondsman who would guarantee his local debts. The surrounding swamps were infested with alligators and mosquitoes, but progress was being made to civilize the area.

The Baron de Pontalba was happy that despite changes in city proprietorship, the French culture was still alive in his dear city. New Orleans had been dubbed "American Paris" because of its bonds with France in letters, fashion, commerce, and culture. He was hurrying through the Place d'Armes, the center square of the French Quarter that contained the few public buildings. The Presbytere or priest's house and the Cabildo housing the city council were under construction.

The baron skirted past the Spanish church and glanced at the two pillories, wooden gallows where many slave owners punished their slaves in the open for all to see. He headed down Royal Street towards the intersection of St. Peter. He hurried as he neared the "small" theater in the center of the oldest part of the French Quarter. He didn't want to be late.

This Sunday afternoon, May 22, 1796, for the first time in his city—in fact, for the first time in any American city—an opera would make its debut. In New Orleans, unique for its time, shops were open on Sundays, musicians played in the streets, and markets were crowded. Theatrical performances typically drew large audiences. Citizens attended mass in the morning and then socialized in the afternoon. These "recreational Sundays" often shocked non-Catholic visitors. Naturalist and painter John James Audubon noted: "The Levee early was Crowded by people of all Sorts as well as Colors, the Market, very abundant, the Church Bells ringing and the Billiard Balls Knocking, the Guns heard all around. What a Display this is for a Steady Quaker of Philadelphia or Cincinnati."

The theater at 732 St. Peter Street, midway between Royal and Bourbon Streets, was soon in sight. It was a low, two-story brick building with a narrow wrought-iron balcony, so typical of Spanish decor. The baron called the theater "Le Spectacle," but he knew the Spanish citizens called it "El Coliseo." Though New Orleans was culturally French, it was now legally a Spanish territory. But the actors were French liberty lovers who often surprised the Spanish authority by injecting revolutionary ideas and songs into their performances. The Americans would later refer to this playhouse as the St. Peter Street Theater.

The baron was hoping for a breeze this afternoon; indoor performances could be stifling, even when the floor-to-ceiling pairs of wooden doors were thrown open wide to the street to capture any air circulation. He entered the darkened theater and looked around for his special box seat on the lower floor of the theater. Balcony seats, set high and back from the front stage, were for free blacks and nonwhites. He looked around for the Spanish mayor's representative who would keep order, prohibiting insults or antigovernment rabble.

Monsieur Louis Tabary looked out at the paying patrons seated in his theater. He thought back to his exile in Santo Domingo after he had fled the violence of the French Revolution and his recent struggle to escape the slave uprising that had just taken place there. He along with many others had immigrated to New Orleans to start a new life. The city had nearly doubled in size as refugees flooded the expanding town. They brought their heritage with them, making significant contributions to the changing culture. Tabary had worked hard to establish himself in the new, strange city. He was a grand actor in the commedia Italiano tradition who loved what he did best. Little did he know that his small band of six actors, singers, and musicians would be so welcomed. For several years he had entertained the people of New Orleans with street performances and had put on productions in abandoned shops and tents set up around the city. He had finally been able to buy the Theatre St. Pierre playhouse from the Perisien brothers. It had been a good decision, he thought, though pressing monetary and management issues constantly plagued him. Fortunately, he had gotten some help from the government, receiving subsidies from public dance halls and post-performance dances to help pay his orchestra.

The baron sat still in his seat, anxious for the production to begin. The performance was well-attended as usual, and everyone began to settle in their seats. It was to be an opera-comique, and he had heard that this type of work had been gaining in popularity in France. He couldn't wait to write to his wife, the baroness, who had left the city with their son to escape the summer heat and threat of cholera. He would give her a full report of the production.

His heart raced as the orchestra tuned its instruments. Tonight's production, *Sylvain,* was based on *Erast,* a drama by Solomon Gessner, a German-Swiss writer of pastoral idylls. Composer Andre Ernest Modeste Gretry, friend of Voltaire, and Jean-Francois Marmontel, who had written the libretto, had gained renown for their works marked by sweetness and melody, qualities that were warmly appreciated by the citizens of a turbulent era. Premiering in 1770 in Paris, *Sylvain* was acclaimed because of its popular theme of the simple life, where people achieved domestic happiness and the virtues of hard work and parental love paid off.

Impresario Tabary's production would not disappoint his New Orleans audience. As the singers took their positions on stage, the first documented staging of an opera in the country began. In his letter the baron wrote that he was pleased with the production and felt New Orleans had indeed earned her title "Outpost of the Paris Opera." He didn't say if he participated in the singing and dancing that acted as the finale of the performance and usually lasted until 1:00 A.M.

Since 1796 New Orleans has had operatic performances almost annually. In the 1800s more than 400 operas would premiere in New Orleans. For many years, New York and Philadelphia found New Orleans their main rival. To celebrate the Louisiana Purchase Bicentennial in 2003, Thea Musgrave was commissioned to write a historical opera. She based her work, *Pontalba,* on the colorful local character, Baroness de Pontalba, who had married the son of the baron who had attended the first opera and written the documented letter to his out-of-town wife. In tribute to that first opera, Musgrave used a dance from *Sylvain* in *Pontalba,* at the beginning of act 1, scene 1. When the harpsichord started playing, the oldest composition performed in the city and the newest opera to be presented joined together to create a unique musical experience for New Orleans theatergoers.

THE STARS AND STRIPES WAVE OVER THE CITY

- 1803 -

Governor Manuel de Salcedo and the Marques de Casa Calvo, representatives of Spain, sat across the table from French Prefect Pierre Clement de Laussat in the Sala Capitular, the grand chamber of the Cabildo, the seat of Spanish government in New Orleans. Laussat presented his papers of authority from Napoleon. The Spanish grandees placed the keys to the city's forts on a silver platter and handed it to Laussat. The Spanish governor then went to the balcony overlooking the Plaza de Armas and rescinded the people of Louisiana from allegiance to the Spanish king. A single cannon shot was fired over the Mississippi River, and the Spanish anthem was played for the final time. The crowd watched in pouring rain as the Spanish flag was lowered. The French tricolor flag was raised in its place.

After forty years of Spanish rule, on November 30, 1803, the Louisiana Territory was turned over to France. There was much celebration of the event. Laussat, the French envoy, was wined and dined by prominent New Orleanians. Bernard Philippe de Marigny de Mandeville, the golden boy and bon vivant of Creole life, gave lavish dinner parties and arranged fireworks displays at his house by the levee.

Laussat took possession of the Louisiana Territory in New Orleans, but something was amiss. New Orleanians were confused by the slow change to French rule. Then came stunning news: Napoleon had sold Louisiana to the United States. Laussat was supposed to have turned Louisiana over to the United States the day after receiving it from Spain, but he didn't. He wanted France to control the grand port city and called the sale "a false transfer." When the Spanish authorities were ousted, he took over as governor and created a new council responsible to France.

Laussat was not alone in wanting France to govern the city; many New Orleanians did not wish to be a part of the United States. Founding fathers had been successful in relegating the English-speaking Americans to the newer, uptown area of the city, far from the French Quarter. Old families still forbade English to be spoken in their homes and sought to keep the Americans at arm's length, despite the fact that the city's trade and economy had been spurred by their business interests.

Those who saw the writing on the wall decided to welcome the second transfer of Louisiana to the United States. There was more celebration. Laussat, now resigned to the transfer, held a "fete to the French flag," Spaniards held fiestas, and Marigny again rolled out the gilded carpet. At a late-night party the evening before the treaty was to be signed, representatives of all countries engaged in dinner, cards, dancing, and a 3:00 A.M. supper. Toasts were made to Spain, France, and the United States, each ending with a twenty-one-gun salute.

Although there was triumph in the air, American officials who made their way to New Orleans were very nervous.

The sale was circumspect and disputed. Napoleon had forced

Spain to return Louisiana because he wanted to stop the westward expansion of the United States while securing a supply post for his French West Indies colonies. President Thomas Jefferson found out about the deal with Spain and, sensing an opportunity to establish U.S. trade rights on the Mississippi River, sent Robert Livingston to France to try to buy New Orleans. Napoleon refused.

Napoleon had planned to send soldiers stationed in the West Indies to secure a French New Orleans. But a successful slave revolt in Saint-Domingue (present-day Haiti) spoiled these plans, and his troops were ousted from the islands. No longer needing to supply the islands, Napoleon recalled his men to France instead of sending them to New Orleans.

Jefferson again saw a chance to acquire New Orleans and sent James Monroe to negotiate a deal. But before Monroe got to France, Napoleon offered to sell not just New Orleans but the entire Louisiana Territory to the Americans. Napoleon's minister of treasury, the Marquis de Barbe-Marbois, negotiated with Livingston and Monroe for a price of $15 million. The territory, from Canada to the Gulf of Mexico and from the Mississippi River to the Rocky Mountains, was had for the bargain price of 4 cents an acre.

Spain was furious over the sale and would have liked to have bought the territory for herself. In fact Spain had been told that the sale to the Americans was just for show and that Napoleon would actually sell Louisiana to Spain for $2 million.

Jefferson was criticized by his opponents for being duped by Napoleon and wasting $15 million on territory described as "a wilderness unpeopled with any beings except wolves and wandering Indians." Federalist newspapers called it "idiotic folly." When Jefferson heard from Livingston that Napoleon might withdraw his offer if the treaty was not signed immediately, Jefferson acted quickly. He chose not to amend the U.S. Constitution in a lengthy process and instead put the treaty before Congress on the grounds of national security. He pointed to the need to remove France from U.S. shores. After a short debate, on October 20, though Louisiana was still in Spanish hands, the treaty with France was ratified by a vote of twenty-four to seven. Many politicians called the acquisition unconstitutional.

Nearly all French citizens along the Mississippi were disgruntled that their homeland was being passed into the hands of the Americans.

Fearing an armed resistance from various fronts, Jefferson appointed William C. C. Claiborne, former governor of the Mississippi Territory, and General James Wilkinson as American representatives to receive the territory from the French officials. Claiborne and Wilkinson arrived in Louisiana with 400 regular troops and 100 Mississippi militiamen.

On December 20, 1803, Claiborne and Wilkinson, escorted by armed forces, were received by Laussat in the Cabilido's Sala Capitular. Just twenty days after it had been raised, the tricolor flag of France was lowered and replaced by the Stars and Stripes of the United States. The Plaza de Armas had been renamed the Place d'Armes and now would be called by its Anglo name, the French Quarter. French citizens wept openly. Americans in attendance sang Revolutionary War victory songs.

At the closing dinner that followed the transfer, four toasts were given. The first was made to the United States and Jefferson with Madeira wine; the second was made to Charles IV of Spain with Malaga wine; another was made to France and Napoleon with champagne; and a last toast was made to the future happiness of the Louisiana Territory, which would eventually be divided to make up all or part of fifteen states.

Jefferson chose twenty-eight-year-old Claiborne as governor of the Territory of Orleans. The Cabildo today houses the Louisiana State Museum, where Napoleon's bronze death mask, one of four known existing masks, is on display.

THE SCALES OF JUSTICE ARE SLIGHTLY TILTED

- 1830 -

ANTEBELLUM NEW ORLEANIANS PARTICIPATED IN mysterious rituals that had roots in faraway places like West Africa and Haiti. Slaves used protective charms of pierced coins and crystal pendants to ward off evil and tried to control their masters with powerful amulets. The whites, too, visited voodoo high priests and queens to put curses on enemies or succeed in love with potions and spells. Rich ladies paid exorbitant prices for gris-gris trinkets that would hasten good luck. Both blacks and whites participated in the ritualistic orgies that took place throughout the city, both publicly and secretly. Police reports reveal that white ladies were often found dancing with black worshippers drinking *tafia* in feverish St. John's Eve celebrations.

It was in this environment that a wealthy Creole gentleman of a prominent New Orleans family turned to magic to help him with a serious situation. His only son had been arrested for a crime that, of course, he did not believe his son capable of committing. There was strong evidence against his son, however. In fact, the man's attorney said the case seemed lost and conviction was almost certain. The man was confused and desperate.

He turned to the occult to help his son and set out to visit Marie Laveau, the undisputed queen of voodoo. To most outsiders Marie Laveau was a hairdresser, but she was above all else a powerful voodoo priestess. She reigned over the exotic rituals held on the banks of Bayou St. John and conducted ceremonies near her Milneburg cottage on Lake Pontchartrain. She was known for her frenetic and seductive dances with her snake, Zombi, who was said to possess his own supernatural powers. She had the gift to charm and curse and could even cause people to die. The man was hoping that she could save his son from the hangman's noose.

The frantic father knocked urgently on the door of Marie's modest home in the 1900 block of Rampart Street, the house Marie's rich father, Charles Laveau, had given her as a dowry when she married Jacques Paris. The gentleman begged the tall, statuesque woman standing before him to save his son's life. Marie, a mixture of black, Indian, and white, with skin that shone with a reddish hue, looked at the man with fierce black eyes. Her curly black hair was held in a *tignon,* a kerchief tied tightly around her head with seven knots. She wore big gold hoops in her ears and gold bracelets on her arms. She did not turn the well-dressed white man away.

When Marie asked for the details of the case, the man explained that his son had been accused of murdering a young girl in a fit of passion. He loved his son dearly and would give anything to save his life. The woman listened closely.

Marie, a clever woman who by this time had turned her success as a voodoo queen into a money-making business, quickly assessed the man's offer. She agreed to take the case. What she required in return for getting the young man declared innocent was a fine new house.

The man was elated. Yes, anything to save his son. A house? Of course.

Marie announced the boy would be acquitted and closed the door. The man was shocked at her certainty but felt relieved. He left his son's fate in the woman's hands.

The night before the trial, Marie assembled an odd assortment of several ingredients and put them deep in her gris-gris bag, reciting a short prayer as she did so. As morning broke on the day of the trial, Marie put three guinea peppers in her mouth, grabbed her potion bag, and went to the St. Louis Cathedral. Marie was a devout Catholic who attended church every day and close friend of Pere Antoine, the beloved Capuchin priest.

With the peppers in her mouth, Marie knelt at the communion altar railing for several hours, praying intently. Then she took the peppers out of her mouth and put them in the gris-gris bag. She stepped into the harsh New Orleans sun and scurried to the Cabildo, the government office building and courthouse just a few steps away.

Marie Laveau held absolute control over her believers, often due to the fear tactics she had no compunction about using when she needed a favor. Consequently she could get things done and go places that ordinary people could not. Marie persuaded a worker she knew to let her into the empty courtroom where the trial was scheduled to take place. She reached into her gris-gris bag and took out the still-moist guinea peppers. She ventured to the front of the room and placed the peppers directly underneath the judge's chair. Marie felt her combination of voodoo and Catholic ritual made her incantations powerful.

In just a few hours, the young man's trial began.

One story goes that Marie waited out the trial patiently in the Place d'Armes, the popular public square just outside the Cabildo. Because she had coerced a witness who was deathly afraid of voodoo to testify in favor of the young man, she was confident of the not guilty verdict. Another report says the voodoo queen was in the courtroom during the proceedings. When the district attorney stood up to present his case against the man's son, Marie pulled a strand of hair from her head, folded it into a wad of paper, and threw it at the prosecutor. The paper hit him on the shoulder and suddenly the man became silent, resting the state's case before he had finished presenting the damning evidence. The judge had no choice but to hand down a verdict of not guilty.

Whether Marie was orchestrating the trial from outside or inside the courtroom, one thing is certain. The young man was found innocent and released.

The wealthy man was true to his promise. He presented Marie with a fine house on Rue Ste. Ann in the Vieux Carre between Rue Burgundy and North Rampart Streets, very near Congo Square. The house, hidden behind banana and bamboo trees and a high fence, was the perfect place for the voodoo queen to practice her craft. She lived in this house for fifty years, until her death in 1881. Her reputation for casting and removing spells and predicting futures grew with each success. She cooked up love potions in the outdoor kitchen and held secret meetings at night in the backyard.

Marie helped the wounded at the Battle of New Orleans and showed kindness toward death-row convicts, often lacing their gumbo with comforting medicinal herbs. Her obituary in the *Daily Picayune* praised her life: "She had the cause of the people at heart and was with them in everything. . . . Marie will not be forgotten in New Orleans." She is buried in St. Louis Cemetery No. 1 in the Glapion family vault. Many say that if you draw an X on the side of her tomb, your wish will be granted.

A NEW ORLEANS FISHING TALE

- 1840 -

THROUGHOUT THE FIRST HALF OF THE 1800S, there was no place in America where dueling was more in vogue than New Orleans. Brought to the city by French settlers who sought to protect their honor using swords, pistols, poison pills, and knives, dueling was considered the most chivalrous way to settle a dispute.

Famed Jim Bowie lived in New Orleans, where he and his brother traded slaves with the infamous pirate Jean Lafitte. In 1827 Bowie pulled his trusty butcher knife out in a duel and gave birth to the bowie knife. Because of his considerable skill with the lethal blade, he was considered the South's most respected knife fighter. Soon blacksmiths were being asked to duplicate the big bowie blade, and it, too, became a popular dueling weapon.

The arrangement of a duel was a civilized act and followed the code duello, a document formed in 1777 in Ireland. It contained twenty-six rules for a proper duel: time of day, number of shots for satisfaction, weapon choice, etc. Duels usually ended with the first drawing of blood, and each combatant had a "second" whose job was to bring the two gentlemen together without violence and attend to the rules.

Gentlemen in New Orleans were often challenged to duels, and the city was reputed to have hosted more duels than any other place in the country. Spurred by excessive vanity, men often challenged one another for a slight mishap, ridicule, or affront to them or their loved ones. A duel was once fought over an insulting remark a European made in reference to the Mississippi River, when he called it a "mere brook." Upon hearing such disrespect, a New Orleanian gentleman slapped the commentator's face and the duel was set.

At this time the most famous dueling place was the pair of Duelling Oaks located on the edge of town, now City Park. Laden with the legendary Spanish moss, they were part of an ancient 600-year-old forest. Under these magnificent oaks was the "field of honor" where many duels took place. The sprawling limbs reached out nearly twice the height of the tree and witnessed as many as ten duels a day eagerly attended by 200 to 300 spectators.

The *Times-Democrat* of New Orleans reported, "Between 1834 and 1844 scarcely a day passed without duels being fought at the Oaks. Why it would not be strange if the very violets blossomed red of this soaked grass!" The leaves of the Duelling Oaks were readying themselves for still another showdown.

Captain S. M. Harvey journeyed to New Orleans in 1840, leaving behind his illustrious whaling career. He settled into the southern way of life and eventually married into a prominent family by wedding Miss Louise Destrehan. One evening he and his wife attended a fancy dinner party. It was followed by a gentleman's card game, which was the custom in antebellum South. The game, however, got heated, and a disagreement arose between Harvey and a Creole gentleman, Albert Farve. In response to some provocation, Harvey, not versed in the subtleties of Creole self-control and the importance of defending one's honor, punched Farve in the face. Farve was knocked to the ground and suffered a black eye. The next day, Farve's second arrived to challenge Harvey to a duel "on the field of honor."

As the one challenged, Harvey was advised that according to the code duello rules he could "choose his weapon." Further explaining the situation, Farve's second continued, "You, sir, may select pistols, swords, rifles, shotguns or any dangerous weapon in which you may be skilled."

Harvey did not want to duel the aggrieved Farve, especially over a card game, but he, too, had his honor to protect. He accepted the challenge to duel Farve on the terms the second had just presented and inquired as to the time and place.

Harvey had called upon his ingenuity and had come up with a way to save his honor and life. (Had he heard that Abraham Lincoln had suggested cow dung as the "weapon of choice" when challenged by another attorney?)

When the second asked Harvey which weapon he should tell Farve had been chosen, Harvey certainly had to stifle a smile. He told Farve's second that his weapon of choice would be his 10-foot, hickory-handled whaling harpoons.

As to the question of these being "dangerous weapons," Harvey led Farve's second to his backyard. He walked off the requisite twenty paces, then lifted the harpoon over his shoulder. He pulled back his arm and let the harpoon sail unswervingly toward the tree just ahead. Upon impact, the tree was split in half.

Farve's second is reported to have asked, "What, sir, do you suppose my friend to be, a fish to be struck by such a damn tool as that?"

Harvey answered, "Fish or no fish, this is my choice of weapons."

The second promptly returned to Farve and related the captain's skill with the whaling harpoon. After careful deliberation, Farve decided he had not really been insulted by Harvey during the card game after all.

Dueling in New Orleans died down after the Civil War. Weary battlefield participants finally viewed it as an unacceptable way to settle differences. Laws were passed to outlaw duels, though the practice continued. The last duel under the Duelling Oaks of City Park occurred on June 22, 1889, when H. S. Salvant met E. J. LeBreton. At 5:00 A.M. as the duel began, a milkman heard shots ring out and awakened a policeman living close by. He stopped the duel, arrested the participants, and placed both of them under a $100 peace bond.

Today City Park contains the largest collection of mature live oaks in the world, some several hundred years old. Their preservation is guarded by the Friends of City Park. Unfortunately, only one of the Duelling Oaks remains; the other died in the 1940s.

A SMALL BOY LOOKS INTO HIS FUTURE

- 1845 -

THE MILD DECEMBER DAY WAS FILLED WITH EXCITEMENT. New Orleanians loved competition, and they clamored around the table where the game to determine the first U.S. champion of chess was about to begin. As it was a Monday, the streets and cafes were crowded with businessmen making their way from Canal Street, the center of retail trade, to Jackson Square via Exchange Alley, a small busy lane sandwiched between Royal and Chartres Streets. Exchange Alley connected the massive block-long St. Louis Hotel to the French Quarter and its government buildings and got its name from the numerous coffeehouses or "exchanges," actually taverns, found there. Citizens of the fourth largest port in the world regularly imbibed strong coffee as well as wine, beer, rum, brandy, and fine liqueurs from Europe during the day. Talking business was important in the waterfront marketplace, and the New Orleans directory listed more than 500 "coffeehouses."

Over the past few years, chess had been gaining in popularity around the world, and in the Crescent City the game would be taken to a new level. Though still ruled by the masters of the wealthy and privileged classes, it found its way into the coffeehouses and would soon become a game of the populace.

The first U.S. championship competition was set to begin in Exchange Alley. Charles Stanley, one of the best English players, had immigrated to America two years earlier. He had begun a regular newspaper column on chess in the influential the *Spirit of the Times,* the first in the United States. He had learned from the best in England, and at eighteen he had defeated chess master Howard Staunton in a pawn-and-two-move handicap match. In New York he had beaten every opponent at the chess club of which he was secretary. He was the organizing force behind the present competition and one of the two participants.

The lozenge-shaped room of the large Sazerac Coffeehouse, where twelve bartenders served customers throughout the day, was colorfully decorated. Sazerac cocktails, a concoction created by a local French Quarter pharmacist, Dr. Antoine Amadie Peychaud, were being mixed and poured for the thirsty patrons. Sazerac cocktails had spread in popularity to the city's finest coffeehouses, but the name was always strongly identified with the Sazerac Bar at 13 Exchange Alley, owned and operated by Sewell Taylor. The chessboard sat atop a small dark-brown table, and the inanimate white and black chessmen were waiting patiently on their home squares. The gaming tables were quieted. The match was set to go. This first recognized match for the U.S. championship was also the first organized chess event in the United States and the first event ever held for the sole purpose of recognizing the best player in the United States; the title of U.S. champion did not yet exist. The match rules stated that the first player to win fifteen games would be declared the U.S. champion.

Stanley had an effervescent personality and was well liked because of his grace in defeat as well as victory. Despite his proclivity for heavy drinking, Stanley was a gentleman in all circumstances; he also displayed a charming humor and ready wit. But with all these accomplishments, Stanley was still the challenger; Eugene Rousseau of New Orleans was recognized as the strongest player in the country. Rousseau had also immigrated to the United States, arriving from France three years prior, a year before Stanley. Rousseau, a distant relation of French philosopher Jean Jacques Rousseau, had settled into the colorful life of the New Orleans Chess Club. He had defeated Benjamin Oliver and John W. Schulten and had suffered a painfully close loss in a hundred-game match against Lionel Kieseritsky in 1839.

The match soon became a symbolic battle of North against South and attracted much attention not just in New Orleans but across the country. The winner-take-all stakes were high. (Divided purses would not occur until nearly forty years later.) One man would walk away with $1,000. The first to win fifteen games, not counting draws, would be crowned champion. Stanley was white in the odd-numbered games. The match began, and the clock clicked away. There were no time limits on the plays; such limitations were still years away. Stanley started out strong, winning the first three games; then Rousseau managed a draw in the fourth game. He was coming back strong, and games five, six, and eight went to Rousseau. Stanley had won number seven. After eight games of play the score stood Stanley, four; Rousseau, three; with one draw. Stanley won games nine through twelve; game thirteen was a draw, as was game fourteen. Stanley took game fifteen, and Rousseau inched out wins on games sixteen and seventeen. Game eighteen went to Stanley, and nineteen went to Rousseau; twenty was a draw. Rousseau seemed to rebound and won game twenty-one, but games twenty-two and twenty-three were draws.

After twenty-three games of play, tensions were high. As the afternoon lengthened, the crowd continued to grow. There was a young boy in the crowd, only eight years old, who never tired of watching the players making their moves across the chessboard. He was the nephew of Rousseau's "second," a native of the city himself, present to make sure the rules of fair play were followed and to give strategic advice if needed. The man was a strong player himself and a well-known chess analyst and had brought the boy along, allowing him to watch the games in the "coffeehouse." The boy peered intently, craning his neck to see past the bodies in front of him. The score stood Stanley, ten, Rousseau seven, with six draws. Game twenty-four went to Stanley, twenty-five was a draw, and twenty-six went to Stanley. Rousseau countered by winning game twenty-seven, and twenty-eight was a draw. At game twenty-nine Stanley needed still three more games to achieve the fifteen required to be named the victor. He was up to the challenge. By winning games twenty-nine, thirty, and thirty-one, Stanley finished Rousseau off and won the match with the required fifteen wins. He had sustained eight losses and eight draws. He was the first U.S chess champion.

Stanley would go on to write a book of the 1845 match called *Thirty-one Games at Chess, Comprising the Whole Number of Games Played in a Match Between Mr. Eugene Rousseau, of New Orleans, and Mr. C. H. Stanley, Secretary of the New York Chess Club.* And that's exactly what the book was.

The young boy, though hardly noticed by the raucous men of the Sazerac Bar, was making his own history that day. He had studied the games and could recall each and every move. The boy had a lot to think over on the walk back to his French Quarter home with his Uncle Ernest Morphy. The opening move in games six and sixteen was especially interesting, he thought, and he planned to use that play in a game with his uncle soon.

That young boy would meet Charles Stanley in match play in 1857 at the First American Chess Congress in New York, when he was just twenty years old, and easily take away Stanley's hard-won title. The boy's name was Paul Morphy, and he would not only become the second U.S. champion but would also be hailed by the entire chess world as "the greatest player that ever lived." And that opening move of Stanley's that so concerned young Morphy? He would fully perfect this strategy to defend a classical king-pawn opening, and that move today is called the Morphy Defense.

BRONZE JOHN, AN UNWELCOME VISITOR

- 1853 -

As summer approached, New Orleans residents became fearful, listening and watching for any signs of the deadly visitor. Those who could afford to were looking forward to their annual trips up north or abroad where the summer temperatures were milder. But despite a booming economy, most citizens would be unable to leave. July's hot and humid temperatures enfolded the city in a sauna, but the political scene was quiet and business was thriving. The largest cotton crop to date was on the market, and the sugar-cane industry was prospering.

The first victim of 1853 was an Irish fellow who had recently arrived in the city to work. He was taken to the doctor after emitting a black vomit. Bronze John, yellow jack, the saffron scourge, or yellow fever, as the disease was called, attacked a victim's stomach lining, causing violent retching.

When other victims followed, the disease was traced to the *Augusta, Siri, Camboden Castle,* and *North Hampton,* ships that had arrived in port in mid-May. These early cases did not yet sound an alarm, and the local press hesitated to report on the scourge at all. Although there were nine deaths during the third week of June, those who could have spoken up about the impending crisis did not. Mentioning that the unsanitary conditions in New Orleans might be the cause of the reccurring disease meant disloyalty to the city. As most of the deaths occurred among immigrants in crowded tenements, New Orleanians turned a blind eye to the problem.

By the end of July, the city was in the grip of the worst yellow-fever epidemic in history. More than a third of the town's 150,000 residents had evacuated, now hoping to escape the danger rather than the heat. Those who stayed behind tended the sick and afflicted, turning the entire city into a hospital. The streets were quiet and deserted save for the occasional hurried footsteps of medical practitioners and the slow roll of carriage wheels transporting the dead to cemeteries.

The suffering was unbearable. The first sign of infection resembled that of an ordinary cold. Victims complained of head- and backaches. Then the disease attacked the liver, the eyes yellowed, and the skin jaundiced. Patients experienced rapidly rising fever, vomiting, urinary blood, and bleeding gums. A victim could fall ill one morning and be dead the following day. Others could linger in the throes of misery for weeks before death. Some would manage to survive.

The city tried to stop the disease from spreading. Thinking that a poisonous ill wind blew in from the swamps and bred in the filthy city streets, the board of health fired cannon throughout the city to drive away the yellow-fever wind, the "miasma."

Churches forbade traditional Catholic funeral services from July 1 to December 1, fearing family members and congregations would be exposed to the disease. Chapels were set up beside cemeteries to bless victims before they were put in the ground. Our Lady of Guadalupe Chapel was erected beside St. Louis Cemetery No. 1 and Father James

Lesne of the Saint Jude Mortuary Chapel performed services for the parishioners of the Saint Louis Cathedral in the Vieux Carre.

The Howard Association, a group of young men founded by Virgil Boullemet, aided outbreak victims by setting up temporary hospitals and convalescent facilities. William L. Robinson, a Howard member, described the epidemic in his diary saying "the putrid exhalations were sickening."

August started off badly: 1,186 people died the first week. On August 24, the black day of the outbreak, 230 deaths were reported, the most in a single day.

Many orphanages were erected to care for the children left homeless, including the Protestant Orphans Home on Magazine Street. Margaret Haughery became known as an angel of mercy. After the deaths of her husband and daughters from yellow fever, she devoted herself to working with the Sisters of Charity and caring for the city's orphans. Charity Hospital helped the city's poor, providing health care and burial plots in Cypress Grove II. Mass burials were conducted in the Girod Cemetery, and one site there is known as Yellow-Fever Mound.

Callers crying "bring out your dead" roamed the streets ready to carry fresh corpses away. But because the Catholic Church didn't allow cremation, bodies began to pile up at the cemeteries. These "Cities of the Dead" were like miniature cities of aboveground tombs and vaults complete with doors, windows, roofs, and decorative motifs. The demand for grave diggers was so great that laborers were offered $5.00 an hour to bury the dead.

The *New Orleans Daily Crescent* described an August day at one of the cemeteries: "Inside there were piles by the fifties, exposed to the heat of the sun, swollen with corruption, bursting their coffin lids . . . what a feast of horrors."

In an effort to contain the disease, many corpses were buried in shallow mass graves, and lime was mixed in with the dirt to help decay the bodies quickly.

When shooting off cannon, banning religious burial rites, and throwing lime in mass burial sites didn't stop the epidemic, citizens were given tar pots to burn in their yards to smother the disease. The city itself set up barrels of tar at distances of 150 feet along Canal, Rampart, and Esplanade Streets to disinfect the air. The evening sky filled with glowing dense smoke curling from the tar pots. The sickness paid no heed to the funereal pall that hung over the city.

A report carried from New Orleans by the SS *Sierra Nevada* spoke of the "dreadful mortality in New Orleans." It said, "At times the dead could not be buried as fast as they were taken to the cemetery. At one time there were forty bodies exposed, uninterred, in Lafayette Cemetery, in the morning, and at sundown, had increased to eighty."

It estimated that, by the end of August, 200 persons a day were dying of yellow fever.

Locals who had survived earlier epidemics thought they were immune to yellow fever, but this summer even longtime residents had succumbed to the ravages of the awful disease. Citizens who had chosen to stay in the city changed their minds and decided to leave. They feared death was knocking too close to their door. But many who left were unknowingly already infected and spread the disease to outlying areas before they died. The obituaries of many New Orleanians were carried in newspapers across the South.

Yellow fever is carried by a mosquito, *Aedes aegypti,* and it would be almost fifty years before scientists would identify the virus that causes the disease. The city's open-air sewage gutters, filthy streets, surrounding swamps, and stagnant water pools were perfect breeding ground for the disease-carrying mosquitoes. The number of deaths in the 1853 epidemic is estimated at more than 10,000.

EXPOSING MORE THAN THE TRUTH

- 1853 -

The courtroom was crowded to capacity. Every sector of the city was represented from yeoman to gentry. A "cause celebre" would be heard by Recorder Winter today.

Just a few days ago, Lola had arrived with a flourish at the St. Charles Hotel for her engagement in New Orleans at the Varieties Theatre on Gravier Street. Many had turned out to greet her, hoping to catch a glimpse of the femme fatale whose rakish reputation had already circulated throughout the city. Some playful young men had commandeered a band and congregated around the entertainer singing love songs. Puritanical oglers booed and hissed. Melees ensued and challenges were meted out for duels. It would be an exciting theater season.

Lola Montez was an infamous "danseuse" who, though already married to an Englishman, had used her womanly wiles on the owner of France's largest newspaper to give a publicity boost to her career. When that love affair died down, she had wooed and won

King Ludwig of Bavaria, who had made her a countess and built her a palace. Fleeing the disapproval of the Bavarian people, she was reported to have used a knife in anger, slashing George Trafford Heald, an army officer she had subsequently married. Disgraced by her arrest due to the discovery of her bigamist relationship with Heald, as she had never legally divorced the Englishman she had married years earlier, she skipped bail and sailed to America. Now she was driving the public wild with her Spider Dance.

Some say her bizarre gyrations were based on an Italian dance that had been the rage for years. To many it was a repulsive dance; to others it was pure erotica. *The New Orleans Bee* had called her dance "the poetry of motion."

You can judge for yourself from the *Bee*'s description:

> *. . . her long slender legs in flesh-colored tights . . . her skirt consisted of tiers of tinted chiffons creating the illusion of a spider's web, entrapping her as she spun around . . . she struggled to free herself and shake off the spiders lurking in her chiffons. As the dance grew more frantic she shed the spiders and stamped then* [sic] *underfoot. . . . Lola spread out her hands and feet like a spider and leaped from one side of the stage to another. . . . It all ended with fire and abandon, as she stamped on the last of the fallen spiders.*

Theatergoers enjoyed the nightly spectacles, but many, turned away from sold-out performances, had to settle for conversation and speculation at the Falcon Coffee House next door.

Lola had already skirted scandal in New Orleans. The first major incident was during her act when she felt she was not getting the attention she deserved. Stopping the show, she haughtily approached the footlights and shocked New Orleans patrons by threatening to cease her performance if the small group of people down front did not stop talking immediately. The crowd went berserk, stomping, cheering, and begging her to carry on with shouts of "Bravo, Lolly!" Showers of bouquets were thrown to her feet from all sections of the theater.

Then the *New Orleans Delta* and the *Boston Daily Mail* reported the seductress's brush with law enforcement for failure to pay wages to her servant. Lola called upon her position as a countess to plead her innocence and privilege, whereupon the two New Orleans policemen announced that no title could exempt one from the law. Attempting to defend her honor herself, Lola grabbed a dagger and brandished it about. The officers were able to overcome the egotist and remove the weapon, but not before she sunk her teeth into their hands and arms.

Then in a dramatic gesture, the countess grabbed a vial of poison, and when she had emptied the contents announced, "Now I shall be free from all further indignity!"

Lola fainted directly and the officers, fairly certain death was not imminent, left her in the care of her friends, who promised to get her to the station the next day. Subsequently the wages were paid to the maid and no court action was taken. The poison was, of course, harmless.

The incident now before the court had occurred just a week before during a Dramatic Fund benefit at the Varieties Theatre. The flamboyant performer had had an altercation with the theater prompter, George J. Rowe. She had accused him of making an improper advance and had kicked his leg. He had kicked back. Lola proceeded to call the manager a d—d scoundrel, a d—d liar, and a d—d thief. He sued her for assault and battery.

Arriving at the courthouse, Lola was ready for a spirited performance. A woman of slight stature, she sailed down the Hall of Justice, past anxious eyes eager to catch the first glimpse of the intrepid heroine. She entered the courtroom "skipping like a gazelle." Her unforgettable bright black eyes could scarcely conceal the delight of the battle ahead.

When Lola's insults to the proprietor were itemized in the suffocating courtroom, Lola announced their truth: "Ah, my dear fellow, that's just what you are."

Laughter erupted. When she remarked to the judge that he should have charged the packed courtroom admission, he himself was amused. When Lola defended herself against the inflicted kick, she retorted that she had been kicked by a horse before, but never by a donkey, referring to Rowe. The sarcastic remarks drew hoots and guffaws from the crowd, and the atmosphere in the court was reported to be "more like a theatre than a temple of justice."

But the main event was yet to come. Authorities and spectators steeled themselves. Lola was to show the court where Rowe had kicked her. As breaths were sucked in tight, Lola flaunted her way to the middle of the room. With her wit intact and her self-possession evident to all, she slowly put one foot on the table and then pulled herself up. In a tease act, she raised her straw-colored skirts higher and higher. The room fell silent. With one last tug, Lola raised her skirt to a point "well up on her hip," showing off more leg than anyone had paid to see on stage. The men went wild, shouting catcalls and slapping each other on the back. It is said that one man fainted.

Lola triumphantly called for a full and free discharge. Most of the gallants in the room agreed; however, the recorder thought differently and set a trial date. The countess paid a $500 bond and, swinging her thick, shiny hair in the direction of her fans, entered the carriage that would take her back to the hotel.

Lola's last Spider Dance was in 1857. She had performed it more than a hundred times between 1852 and 1857. Her life story became the inspiration for the expression, "Whatever Lola wants, Lola gets," which was composed as a song for the Broadway play *Damn Yankees* in 1955. In her twenty-year career Lola Montez had become the single most talked about woman of her time, and her courtroom antics in New Orleans were reported across the country.

RIDING FOR THE GLORY

- 1854 -

THE METAIRIE TRACK WAS BUZZING AS racing enthusiasts eagerly anticipated what press reports were already calling the "pinnacle of American racing." The elegant country setting and lavish improvements of the thirteen-year-old racetrack had enticed the city's elite with luxurious facilities, new grandstands, and rich purses. Promoter Richard Ten Broeck had taken great pains to ensure that the event would go smoothly, enforcing a respectful "code of behavior."

The track was still muddy from the heavy rains that had fallen the night before and strong winds that had blown across the course turning the mud hard and stiff, but today the weather had cooperated. The New Orleans *Times-Picayune* reported, "Rarely has a lovelier spring day opened to more brilliant hopes and expectations . . . [and] dawned upon the thousands who were rushing forward to the great event of the day."

Most businesses in the city had been suspended, and all roads leading to the Metairie were filled with various means of conveyance.

Newspapers made the significance of the event clear: "The race for everybody and everybody for the race!" Governors and mayors mingled with businessmen and professionals as dinner hours were postponed and engagements were forgotten.

National dignitaries added more drama to the day's activities. Former President Millard Fillmore had journeyed to the Crescent City, saying, "There is no way I would miss this great sporting event." Accompanying him in the judges' stand were Secretary of War Charles M. Conrad and Secretary of the Navy John P. Kennedy.

More than 20,000 spectators filled the Metairie Race Course. Despite the great number of people, a quiet atmosphere prevailed. There would be no drunken displays, no quarrels, and no rude or unruly demonstrations. The only slight ruffle was that though wagering had been heavy and brisk for days, bettors were fearful that they would not be able to place their final bets in time.

The Great State Post Stake was about to begin. It would be a grueling race where horses would be pushed almost beyond endurance for 4-mile heats, in a contest that would take winning two consecutive heats to win. But this would be more than a race of competing thoroughbreds. This would be a heated competition among sister states of the South. A $5,000 entry fee meant that only the best would take the field, only horses worth the money would run. And so there were only four contestants to vie for the ultimate $20,000 purse. Interestingly, three of the entries were half-brothers, all sired by the great racehorse Boston.

On Saturday, April 1, 1854, the boasting rights for the fastest horse were at stake for four neighboring states. Mississippi was represented by Louisiana-bred Lecomte, three-year-old son of Boston. Many thought Lecomte was the fastest thoroughbred in the country. He would be ridden by a jockey known only as John. Kentucky's entry was Lexington, another three-year-old sired by

Boston. Considered Lecomte's equal, the stallion had never lost a race. He would be ridden by Henry Mershon, a sandy-haired Kentuckian who would later become a deputy United States marshal. A rivalry between these two top-notch horses had already developed even before they met on the track.

Louisiana's hope rested on Arrow, a third half-brother sired by Boston. His jockey, listed only as Abe, was a young slave who later became a free man. Abe Hawkins, considered the first African-American professional athlete, went on to enjoy jockey fame and handsome pay. Alabama's entry was Highlander, a seasoned stallion and race contender. His jockey was Gilbert Patrick, often called Gilpatrick, who would enjoy a forty-year riding career.

The competitors pranced proudly to the starting line in front of the judges' stands, showing off their racing prowess. When the drum sounded, the horses were off to the cheers of a frenetic crowd.

Throughout the first mile the horses stayed close together, but coming out of the first turn Lexington, a blazed-faced bay, took the lead with Arrow in second; Lecomte, a sprightly chestnut, in third; and Highlander at the rear. As the stallions began the second mile, Lecomte forged ahead and passed Lexington. The crowd went wild. After enjoying his lead for a short distance, Lecomte fell back and the equines soon fell into their earlier positions. With nostrils flaring, they hung on to those positions throughout the third mile.

On the first turn of the fourth mile, Arrow, with thick clumps of mud sticking to his hooves, began to falter under the stress of such a long race. Highlander passed Arrow, taking third position. As they entered the home stretch, Lecomte vied once more for leadership, but Lexington, known for his excellent form and even temper, held on until the end. Lexington won the first heat by three lengths. The Kentuckians were wild with excitement. Lecomte finished second, Highlander was third, and Arrow finished last.

But the race was not over. While the horses were given a breather, bettors rushed to place their wagers on the next heat. It was still anyone's race. Many thought Lexington would be a sure win, but Lecomte fans knew their horse and believed in his ability and stamina. He still had a good chance to win the second heat, pushing the race to a third heat. Alabamians thought Highlander had not fully extended himself in the first heat and therefore had a reserve of energy to use for the second heat. Hometown supporters hoped Arrow would rally after his rest and run a better race.

The second heat started, and true to the expectations of his fans, Highlander did have more to give. He took an early lead on the first turn; Lexington ran second. The four horses stayed together in a pack for most of the first mile, but Lecomte rushed for supremacy and took the lead as the horses entered the second mile. Lexington then moved past Highlander into second. Alabamians were frenzied as Highlander, now third, made a rush at Lexington, trying to get ahead. Highlander nearly passed Lexington, but failed; a short distance after the next turn, he again fell behind. Lecomte, cheered on by the Mississippians, held tightly onto first place, using his 23-foot stride to lead by nearly eight lengths. The fourth and final mile of the grueling heat loomed menacingly ahead as Highlander began to experience visible distress. He gave up his quest for victory near the same spot where Arrow had faltered in heat one.

On the backstretch Lexington went to work. He gradually closed the gap between him and Lecomte. The pace was increasing; the horses were near exhaustion. On the third turn, Lexington caught up with Lecomte, and the two rivals swung in to the home stretch side by side. The anxious crowds cheered wildly as the horses rushed forward, each at full speed. As they passed the judges' stands heading toward the finish line, Lexington pulled ahead ever so slightly. Each horse strained to go faster. In the end it was Lexington who won the second heat and was crowned victor of The Great State Post Stake.

Reporting the race, the *Times-Picayune* said, ". . . the race was an excellent one; its varying chances, its uncertain termination up to the last minute, the severity of the contest, the amount of money at stake, and immense number of persons in attendance, will render it a brilliant event in the racing annals of this country."

A controversy emerged, however. Because of the muddy track conditions, many, especially Lecomte supporters, considered Lexington's victory a fluke. Lexington was called a "lucky mudder." A rematch was demanded.

One week later, a special match race was held. This time Lecomte won the first two heats, setting a record time in the first heat. Lecomte thus gave Lexington his only career defeat.

One year later on April 2, 1855, Lexington raced against Lecomte's time and beat it soundly. On April 14, the two horses ran a "true" race. Lexington won the first heat handily. Lecomte, ailing from colic, was withdrawn from the competition.

It would be the last race for the brothers. Lexington sired 600 foals, including Preakness. Lecomte was sent to race in England, where he got sick and died; his legacy is the Louisiana town of Lecompte named after him. The Metairie Race Course was bought by Charles T. Howard, who turned it into the prestigious Metairie Cemetery.

LIGHT AS AIR

- 1855 -

In January 1855 the New Orleans *Daily Delta* advertised the opportunity for the public to view the sky antics by veteran balloonist Eugene Godard of France. His balloon would take off from the Place D'Armes. First seats were 50 cents; second seats were 25 cents. Godard, who described himself in the ad as "Physician, French Aeronaut, Member of the Academy of Arts and Industrial Trades, Sciences and Belles Lettres, Chief Aeronaut to the Austrian Government," was making a series of ascensions in the Crescent City. His wife and her corps of a hundred seamstresses in temporary factories set up in the train stations of Paris had sewed the colorful balloons.

Godard advertised he had made more than 200 ascensions, so Louis Moreau Gottschalk felt safety was not an issue as he negotiated for a spot on a March 26 balloon ascent. The colorful balloon, holding 26,000 cubic feet of hydrogen and carbonic gas, swayed ever so slightly on its ropes as Godard, the bold aeronaut, climbed into the gondola. Once aloft, Louis relaxed and realized how happy he was to be home in New Orleans again after so long an absence. His childhood home on Rampart Street near Congo Square had allowed him to listen to the forbidden, frenzied music and catch glimpses of the sultry Creoles dancing on Sunday afternoons. New Orleans's local color had become a part of his world-renowned music.

His father had immigrated to New Orleans from London. The oldest of seven children, his young spirit was fueled by a passion for music inherited from a Creole mother. He had lived a life of affluence and adventure. He also reminisced about Grandma Brusle and longtime slave Sally, who had filled his head with the haunting melodies of Haiti and Africa. By the age of seven, before he could even reach the pedals, he was playing the organ at St. Louis Cathedral with his music teacher controlling the stops. At fifteen he played a farewell concert at the luxurious St. Charles Hotel before he left for a classical music education in Paris. After the concert, in a great display of showmanship, he dramatically handed over his victor's wreath, presented to him by the French counsel, to his mother. He would be known after that maneuver for his bold bravado and exaggerated style and temperament. His stylized playing and Creole-inspired compositions gained him attention throughout Europe. Audiences flocked to see the young virtuoso with the outlandish origins. Chopin applauded him, and Victor Hugo complimented his eloquent oratory.

Louis's nostalgia quickly turned to anxiety. Just six minutes after traveling in a northward direction, the balloon began to make an unscheduled descent over the Pontchartrain Railroad. As death stared him in the face, his short life passed before his heavy-lidded, melancholy eyes, orbs that were said to drive the ladies wild. He was a good-looking young man with wavy hair and well-manicured mustache. He was going down in a hot-air balloon.

Thanks to the skill of the pilot, the young man narrowly escaped injury when the wicker gondola crashed on the tracks, barely missing the train en route to the city. The dangerous sport of hot-air ballooning had enticed and excited him; he had made history by becoming the first composer in recorded history to soar into the heavens.

Now, just six days after cheating death, he had put the incident behind him and was going up in the same gondola with the same pilot, a second time. This time as he glanced at the basket gently struggling against its tethers, he had hopes of a smooth flight.

He and Godard entered the gondola together and the balloonist cast off the heavy ballast. The enormous balloon rose gently into the sky. Louis had had a brainstorm for this flight of fancy, not one as grand as Godard's feat of carrying a horse on a platform under the gondola basket or as precarious as performing gymnastic tricks from the basket high in the air, or as ludicrous as jettisoning a parachuted monkey from the balloon as some of the other daredevil balloonists of the day were doing, but a feat that would push young Louis's musical creativity to a new limit.

When Louis jumped aboard the balloon gondola, he took with him a small keyboard instrument called a harmonicon, a recent invention that combined the harmonica with a keyboard and provided stop mechanisms to regulate the wind input. The balloon ascended quickly and Louis was once again enraptured by the magic of flight. He was inspired and put his hands to the harmonicon. He began to play and "improvised ecstatically" as he flew over the Gulf of Mexico. In an act of true "genius," Louis composed his *L'Extase: Pensee poetique,* the first recorded instance of composition in midair.

But if lightening can strike twice in the same place, it did so this day. Again the balloon went out of control, again the ominous railroad tracks came into view as a potential crash site, and yet again a miracle occurred. The veteran aeronaut Godard managed to direct the balloon to safety and avoided being hit by an oncoming train.

Some say the experience was still alive in Gottschalk's soul when he composed the sensuous and humorous opening to *Printemps d'amour, mazurka: caprice de concert pour le piano.* Gottschalk gave the world a unique view of classical music, and his haunting variations would be emulated by some of the greatest musicians in history: Paganini, Chopin, and Ernst. Compared to his contemporaries, he was described in the press as "most spectacular, flashy and finger-numbing." At his final concert in Geneva, a stunned reviewer reported his variations were "filled with the most original and daring caprices, many played on a single hand."

Gottschalk, an American composer and pianist best known for his virtuosic playing and spicy compositions, is known in New Orleans for his piano solo written in the sky over the city. In the years to come, aviator and hot-air balloonist Godard would achieve ultimate recognition as "The Aeronaut of the Emperor," so named by Emperor Napoleon III when in 1870 his now more reliable balloons carried people and messages in and out of besieged Paris.

WHISTLING DIXIE

- 1861 -

The Varieties Theatre had been built in 1849 by the Association Variete as a burlesque and vaudeville venue, and this night it fulfilled that mission as the audience exploded in applause during the playwright's satirical stabs at stuffy American behaviors and mores.

John Brougham's *Pocahontas!: Ye Gentle Savage* was certainly entertaining the robust opening night audience and living up to the rave reviews carried in all the papers. The author himself had prepped his audiences by describing his play as an "original, aboriginal, erratic, operatic, semi-civilized and demi-savage extravaganza."

The celebrated Mrs. John Wood was cast as the main character, Pocahontas, and her troupe of talented actors filled out the cast. But as the audience benignly enjoyed the extravagantly amusing parody, the evening was about to take a decidedly historic turn.

Near the end of the performance, orchestra leader Carlo Patti, older brother of opera diva Adelina, boldly struck up his band. The handsome violinist had just left his beloved Memphis, Tennessee, and was determined to establish a connective chord in the Crescent City, his new home.

The audience looked skittishly around, aware that something unusual was about to happen. Marching to the opening strains of the requisite final song called the "walk around" and singing at the top of their voices, forty female Zouaves paraded in formation and mounted the stage.

Zouaves were originally elite Algerian units of the French army known for their fighting skill and flamboyant uniforms. New Orleans had commissioned its own Zouave troop, and the sight of their uniforms created a stir that swept through the audience. The women were sporting blue-and-white-striped pantaloons cut in the baggy Zouave fashion; dark blue, waist-length Zouave jackets with red trim; red wool fezzes with blue tassels; white canvas leggings; and black leather grieves. New Orleanians were ever so proud of their Zouaves, the French-speaking battalion under Lieutenant Colonel Coppens. The most colorful unit of the Confederate Army was organized and trained in the French model and actually went into battle clad in the Zouave uniform. The 400-strong battalion had been authorized by Jefferson Davis himself and worked out of its headquarters at 61 Customhouse Street in New Orleans.

The women's voices were loud and clear:

Oh, I wish I was in the land of cotton
Old times there are not forgotten
Look away, look away,
Look away Dixieland.

Patti smiled; he thought back to selecting the new song to play this evening. "Dixies Land," a plantation song by Dan Emmett, had been played only in the North up until now. Emmett had composed the tune around the familiar saying, "I wish I was down in Dixie," used by northern circus people who lived as tented wanderers and by late fall were looking to escape the cold weather and head south. Relying on his banjo and fiddle background and his earlier career in the circus, Emmett had composed the rousing tune for a minstrel show in New York.

The women's voices rang out strong and energetic.

In Dixieland where I was born
Early on a frosty morning
Look away, look away,
Look away Dixieland.

Actress Susan Denim, in town after a successful run at the St. Charles Theatre with Mrs. Wood, was leading the New Orleans-style parade, strutting to the lively tune amid shouts and yells from the fired-up audience. The beautiful comedienne Mrs. Wood and her summer troupe of actors, including Mark Smith, M. W. Leftingwell, and John Owens, actor and Varieties artistic director, had been delighted with Patti's choice of "Dixie." Tom McDonough, member of the troupe, had pronounced, "That will do—the very thing; play it to-night."

The Zouaves performed a drill under Carlo Patti orchestration and the audience flared up once again.

The women's voices excited a rush of patriotism.

Oh I wish I was in Dixie,
Hooray, hooray.
In Dixieland I will make my stand
To live and die in Dixie

The crowd went wild and began singing the stirring refrain:

Away, away,
Away down south in Dixie
Away, away,
Away down south in Dixie

Seven encores followed, all demanded by the enthusiastic audience that sang and stomped until they could carry on no longer and the final curtain closed.

The tune of "Dixie" rushed through the southern countryside unchecked. It was whistled in the cotton fields and played on the battlefield. It was sung by the lone banjo player on his front porch and by regiments marching to battle. Adopted by the army and the navy as the voice of Confederate sentiments, it is reported to have "ignited a firestorm that could not be extinguished."

When Phillip Peter Werlein, owner of the prominent music store on Canal Street, heard the tune ringing throughout the city, he immediately wrote Emmett to secure the southern copyright for the piece. But he couldn't wait for the composer's reply. His beloved South desperately needed a "song" to rally troops and stir patriotism for the Confederate cause. He published the song, selling thousands of copies. He would eventually obtain the copyright from Emmett for $600.

"Dixie" would be published in different versions and with many different spellings, but it was the Werlein version that was played at the inauguration of Jefferson Davis, president of the Confederate States of America. It is also documented to be one of Abraham Lincoln's favorite songs; he was enthralled by its lyrics and music. Just days before his assassination, he requested it be played: "I call upon the band to play Dixie. It has always been a favorite of mine, and since we have captured it, we have a perfect right to enjoy it."

Varieties Theatre also hosted the very first rendition of "The Bonnie Blue Flag," another musical standard of the Confederate States, by Irish actor Harry McCarthy, whose stirring performance was accompanied by his sister waving a Confederate flag. Varieties Theatre burned down in 1854 and was replaced by the Gaiety Theatre. Orchestra leader Carlo Patti's actress-wife became famous when a portrait of her was found on the corpse of John Wilkes Booth after he assassinated President Lincoln.

CONFEDERATE SPY SLIPS AWAY AGAIN

- 1863 -

Loreta Velazquez slid past the Union outpost, skirting the Federal pickets. She knew it would take most of the night to cover the 17 miles between New Orleans and the Confederate forces stationed at Franklin. She had to deliver to the post commander vital information that would help her dear South.

Life-threatening situations were not unknown to Loreta. The young woman had fought in several Civil War battles disguised as a valiant soldier named Harry T. Buford. Loreta had flattened her breasts with shields of malleable wire worn under her army shirt, learned to spit on demand, and donned a fake mustache to appear more manly. She had fought as a cavalry officer at Bull Run and served in Tennessee at Fort Donelson. Wounded in a skirmish, she had hidden out in New Orleans, where she was charged with being a spy. Managing to evade the suspicions of the provost marshal, she was, however, arrested for impersonating a man, and unable to refute the accusations, she endured the ten-day sentence and $10 fine as a fair trade for the lesser offense.

Her last action in combat was at the Battle of Shiloh, where she was wounded. An army surgeon detected her disguise, and she fled the battleground, abandoning her beloved army. She again retreated to New Orleans, now occupied by Union forces under the cruel Major General Benjamin F. Butler, and began spying for the Confederacy. Espionage activities were under greater scrutiny than before, and Butler was ever tightening his hold on the city. But Loreta, rather than worry about the increased pressure, was excited by the difficulties ahead of her. She wrote, "It afforded me an immense amount of satisfaction that, in a quiet way, I would be able to accomplish many things for which Butler would have been highly pleased to have strangled me, could he have discovered what I was about." One of Butler's threats, intended to stir up terror in the hearts of would-be spies, was imprisonment on Ship Island, a desolate piece of sand in the Mississippi Sound.

Loreta gave little consideration to the possibility of prison; she had important papers to deliver. Confederate troops were assembled outside the city waiting for news of Union plans being made within. They were ready to take advantage of any weakness and poised to rush in and rescue their beloved city. But getting information beyond city limits meant running the Union lines. The city sat on a narrow strip of land between the Mississippi River and Lake Pontchartrain. Crisscrossed with numerous bayous, marshy grasslands, and other waterways made concealment perilous, but possible. Loreta was swift of foot, but the highway she needed to traverse was fraught with danger. She had given up her male clothing, and wearing skirts slowed her pace more than she would have liked. The night was terribly lonesome and weary for the young woman. More than once during her trip she heard the ominous sounds of alligators splashing into shallow waters as the animals detected her approach, but she chose to ignore the creatures and kept going. The evening was damp and humid, and mosquitoes swarmed her face and throat as she walked. When she stopped to rest, she fought off the buzzing, biting insects with determined zeal, but they left her face and hands swollen and red.

Loreta limped into the army camp by daybreak, tired and mosquito bitten but satisfied that she was about to complete her mission. Footsore and exhausted, she handed the dispatches over to a Confederate soldier who was directed to deliver them to headquarters. The soldier assured Loreta that her instructions would be carried out. Loreta had successfully delivered into Confederate hands secret Union information from in and around New Orleans.

Aware of Butler's savage punishment for those who dared to defy his mandates, Loreta was relieved to be rid of her burden and turned to find some shelter in which to hide during the daylight hours before she could begin the long walk back to the city under the cover of night. Spotting a nearby house, she hoped her presence would not be questioned and her appearance not be criticized.

Loreta need not have worried. She was treated to a fine breakfast by a respectable family. Her dirty clothing was exchanged for clean attire, and her knowing hosts invited her to rest and sleep a while before beginning her midnight trek back to New Orleans. When Loreta awoke that evening, her hosts offered her the services of one of their horses and escorted her as close to the city as was prudent. Dismounting, Loreta made her way past the pickets once again and entered the French Market. She slipped in among the locals and pretended as if she had been doing some early morning shopping. She walked easily past St. Peter Street toward Rampart Street and from there she went to her room to rest.

But while she slept soundly, things were not going well. The Confederate soldier to whom she had entrusted her information had been caught, and her dispatches had been confiscated. Although her name had not appeared on any of the documents, she had been identified as the writer of the communication and a witness had been found who stated he had seen a young woman roaming the lake area.

Loreta was placed under arrest and brought before the much-feared General Butler. He was certainly not very good looking, the woman noticed, and seemed much the tyrant he was reported to be. Loreta vowed to admit nothing unless Butler produced irrefutable proof of her complicity in the usurped dispatches. She knew his methods of interrogation would be crafty, but she was ready. Butler was convinced he had captured the right person and after much ranting and raving, he pronounced Loreta guilty of spying. He was resolved not to let her slip through his fingers. Loreta chose not to answer any of his charges. She was waiting for whatever proof he could produce. But none came. She remained silent.

When Butler saw that he could not force Loreta into admitting her role in transporting the dispatches, he tried another ploy. "Well, madam, you have shown your hand nicely; I have been wanting you for some time past, and I propose to send you to Ship Island."

This threat was followed with more accusations, but Loreta remained calm.

"Are you not guilty?" said Butler, blinking his eyes, and trying to look as savage as possible. His barrage continued, "Do you mean to say that you are not the writer of that letter, or that you did not smuggle it through the lines?"

It was time for the woman to respond. "I don't mean to say anything about it and I don't mean to confess what I didn't do," she said. Butler was infuriated by her coolness. The stubborn woman was sent to a cell in the Custom House pending further investigation.

But Loreta had an ace up her sleeve. Preparing in advance for a crisis such as this, Loreta had purchased British papers, which she kept in a trunk in her room. With the help of a friend, Sergeant B., who took her message to the British Consul, she was eventually freed. For her own safety, as she knew it would not take Butler long to assemble a stronger case against her, Loreta decided to leave New Orleans and applied for a pass. But Butler was not yet finished with his hostage; her pass was denied. Loreta again had to take the risk of running the blockade; but this time it would be particularly risky as she was still under suspicion of being a spy and if she were caught, Butler would surely exile her to Ship Island. She had no choice.

Loreta went down to the lake and petitioned a fisherman to take her across. She would pay him handsomely for his efforts. At the appointed time, she put on two layers of clothing and prepared to leave the city. The night was clear and the boatman was waiting for her. The sail was hoisted and the pair set off across the dark water. Loreta sat in the small boat reliving her life as a Confederate spy and all that she had accomplished. But she was wary of the fisherman's fidelity, and she would take no chances. She planned her next step sitting in that small boat with one hand on a loaded six-shooter, resolved that at the slightest indication of betrayal, she would put it to the man's head. She had no intention of visiting Ship Island.

After the war Loreta wrote *The Woman in Battle,* published in 1876, which fully detailed her experiences as a Confederate soldier and the many people who helped her along the way, including Sergeant B. Records show that more than 400 women served as soldiers during the Civil War and cite more than 80 women killed or wounded in battle.

COLD STORAGE ENHANCES FINE DINING

- 1869 -

TRADE WITH THE NORTH HAD BEEN TOUGH during the Civil War. Because the ice supply from the cold regions had been cut off, keeping meat and other perishables safe for eating in the hot temperatures of the South was impossible. It became imperative that some process be developed to keep food from spoiling. During the war Ferdinand P. E. Carre's invention using ammonia and water as a refrigerant had been brought over from France and shipped through the Union blockade into Mexico and then Texas. The ingenuity of Daniel Livingston Holden, Thaddeus S. C. Lowe, and John Gorrie improved and refined the process. Holden added steam coils and distilled water to produce clean ice and built a sixty-ton-capacity plant in New Orleans. Lowe used carbon dioxide to reach low temperatures, while Gorrie worked on patenting a compressed-air refrigeration system.

After the war, competition for the refrigeration business grew.

Lowe designed a refrigerated ship, the *William Tabor,* in 1868 to travel to the New Orleans market. He employed his own carbon-dioxide machines, which he had developed to inflate the military balloons used during the war. He was able to produce dry ice to preserve the Texas beef he shipped. Lowe's immediate competitor was Henry Peyton Howard, whose steamship, the *Agnes,* was equipped with a cold-storage room that used the refrigeration system patented by Gorrie. Initially Gorrie had developed his refrigeration system to treat victims of the yellow-fever epidemics. He wrongly reasoned that the ice-cold temperatures would heal the disease. Ironically, he had brought his model to be patented to New Orleans years earlier in the hopes of garnering support for his cooling process. But he had had a hard time assembling the prototype. He complained about "defects of mechanical contrivance and unskilled workmanship" in the city, and he also could not find, nor have made, the two thermometers that he needed to provide reliable readings for the demonstration of his process. He left town discouraged but predicting a future when "fruits, vegetables, and meats would be preserved in transit and thereby enjoyed by all." Sadly, he never saw the success his invention would bring; he died in 1855.

By 1869 both Lowe and Howard were vying for the lucrative New Orleans market. Unfortunately for Lowe, the *William Tabor* was too big a ship and needed too much water to dock at the New Orleans wharves, so Howard's *Agnes,* with its 25- by 50-foot refrigerated storage room, became the first ship ever to deliver frozen beef to the banks of the Mississippi River.

The St. Charles Hotel was spruced up and ready to celebrate the historic event. Its stately alabaster columns showed off the elegant Greek revival architectural style that was popular in New Orleans. The first St. Charles Hotel had burned down a few years ago, but the new structure, designed by Isaiah Rogers, was even more extravagant than its predecessor. Just one block off bustling Canal Street where posh St. Charles Avenue took a slight bend, the hotel was touted as one of the largest and most luxurious in the world. It was the social center of the new American community and renowned for using brown sugar to sweeten hot, steaming cups of tea, even for children. A guest wrote, "I am really afraid I shall kill myself with eating if I stay at this first-class hotel much longer . . . the splendid cold ham, roast mutton, turkey, chicken, duck, oysters, and meats of all kinds, greet the eye and stimulate the appetite."

This night the dining hall was splendidly set and the guests eagerly filed in from the spacious lobby anticipating what would certainly be a most memorable dinner. Texas beef was the featured entree, but it wasn't the fare that was significant this evening; it was the means in which the food had arrived in the city.

Earlier in the week curious crowds had lined the banks of the Mississippi River to greet the *Agnes,* a uniquely outfitted steamboat that would solve the problem of keeping foods fresh for long periods of time. The *Agnes* would be transporting refrigerated meat from Texas.

The beef that the people would be dining on at the exclusive St. Charles Hotel on the evening of July 12, 1869, nearly a month after the shipment had left Texas, marked the beginning of a new era in food preservation. Howard arranged the huge banquet to introduce his prominent New Orleans guests to his frozen beef and to celebrate his potential business success.

Howard also had the frozen Texan meat served as meals in hospitals and at other restaurants and hotels throughout the city. The feat of getting frozen meat from the Texas plains to the growing urban center of New Orleans by using nontoxic and nonflammable carbon dioxide established the compressor process of refrigeration as the way to deliver frozen meat to northern cities and eventually to Europe.

The magnificent St. Charles Hotel burned down again in 1894 and was rebuilt in 1896. It closed its dining halls for good and was demolished eighty years later.

"SHE TAKES THE HORNS"

- 1870 -

In 1812 the great Captain Robert Fulton steered his ship, the *New Orleans,* into the port city of the same name. The *New Orleans* became the first steamboat ever to navigate the Mississippi River. She had traveled at 4 miles per hour downstream. Since then competition to tame the mighty, muddy waters had gone "full steam ahead."

Two years later there were twenty-one steamboats servicing the bustling port of New Orleans. Captain Henry Miller Shreve completed a memorable trip from New Orleans to Louisville aboard the *General Washington* in 1817. When he arrived, crowds carried him aloft on their shoulders as a conquering hero and gave him a twenty-five-gun salute to celebrate the record-setting number of days the journey had taken. Shreveport, Louisiana, would be named after this famous steamboat captain.

In 1828 the *Tecumseh* covered in eight days the same distance it had taken the *General Washington* twenty-one days to complete, and in 1843 the *Sultana* made it in just shy of five days. By then the Crescent City would boast the yearly docking of more than 1,200 packet, passenger, and freight steamboats on her banks, and before the century ended more than 4,000 wheelers would lay anchor in the fourth busiest port in the world, New Orleans.

Many people took great interest in the sport of racing steamboats, wagering heavily on which boat was faster than all the rest. At stake for the boats themselves were the "horns," a set of golden deer antlers that would be proudly displayed for all to see. The antlers were much coveted and allowed the owner to brag that his boat had won a speed sprint between two major cities and that the race had been run honestly and in the presence of witnesses.

The year was 1870. The next big race for the horns would pit the brash Captain Leathers against the stoic Captain Cannon. Both men were well known along the Mississippi River for their navigation skills. The race would start in New Orleans and end in St. Louis, 750 miles upriver. The event was publicized from Philadelphia to Europe. Fortunes were wagered, partnerships forged, enemies made. Not only was the press of New York, Boston, and other U.S. cities on hand, but major newspapers in London and Paris had sent reporters to New Orleans to cover the spectacle.

A date for the race was set—June 30.

Captain Thomas P. Leathers of the *Natchez* was a showman at heart. He was reckless and tended toward grandstanding, but the people loved his antics and were excited to cheer the swashbuckling captain on. To win a race, he was not slow to use trickery, as when he threw slabs of bacon fat into the boiler at opportune times to get the steam up or sounded his cannon to frighten an opponent. The 301-foot *Natchez* could dance through the water like a graceful swan to the sound of Leathers blowing the familiar buzzing whistle on the top of one of the tall smokestacks.

Captain John W. Cannon of the *Robert E. Lee* was just as confident that his boat was the fastest. He was a more serious contender, having barely escaped death when his first steamboat, the *Louisiana,* exploded, killing eighty-six people. He had been on the receiving end of Captain Leathers's theatrics before, and determined not to be outdone once again, he stripped his ship of all but essentials, down to the bare hull. Good-bye to draperies, fixtures, and furniture; no doors, windows, or shutters. He even took the glass out of the pilothouse. According to the *New Orleans Daily Picayune,* he carried only a few special passengers and no cargo aboard the 285-foot, 1,456-ton, eight-boiler sidewheeler.

Leathers, eager to make a profit by his trip upstream and always looking to please more of the crowd, carried his regularly scheduled passengers and freight. Then in a show of supreme confidence, he made the flamboyant gesture of accepting the passengers that Cannon had turned away.

Lining the riverbank, crowds stretched their necks to see the beginning of what would be billed the "Greatest Steamboat Race of All." Thousands of New Orleanians had poured into the waterfront area throughout the day. Mule-drawn carts rested idle along the wharf as bedlam broke out among the spectators along the river. Stevedores raised their voices, eager for the race to start. The boats stood poised to begin, and each person egged his favorite captain on to victory. Many were fearful that the boats would not finish the race at all. Steamboats were dangerous. Fires constantly broke out below deck as boilers were stoked beyond capacity, engines often exploded, or errant embers shot out from smokestacks landed on the deck, starting onboard fires. The average life expectancy of a steamboat was eighteen months. But today most looked beyond their worst fears. There were fortunes to be made . . . and lost.

The starting shot was sounded at 5:00 P.M. precisely.

Shouts and yells from the crowds rang out. People waved their hands wildly, sending the boats off in a fitting fashion. The packets began to move, slowly at first and then faster as steam poured from the stacks overhead.

Cannon beat Leathers out of port by four minutes. Spectators along the shore watched the ships for as long as they could. Some dallied long enough to play card games or make side bets on the race, looking to hedge whatever losses they might incur. It was reported that thousands of dollars had passed hands even before the race was completed.

Reporters with stopwatches stood like sentries all along the riverbank to time the boats. As the steamers passed, runners would note the time then rush to telegraph stations to transmit the progress of the race to the waiting world.

There was an exuberant feeling among the citizens that day as the two steamboats battled it out, boilers red hot, steam puffing from chimneys stacked high into the sky, sending sparks hissing into the dark water. Each ship, pushed to go faster, groaned and moaned under the strain.

At Natchez, Cannon was only six minutes ahead of Leathers. At Vicksburg, with the *Natchez* pressing hard, Cannon pulled a sly maneuver. He was able to lash to the steamboat *Frank Pargaud* and get food and supplies without stopping. By Memphis, the *Lee* was an hour ahead of the *Natchez.* Hundreds of fires lit the night sky on the bluffs along the river so people could watch the race. By midnight no boat could claim a decisive lead.

In New Orleans, race festivities continued day and night as progress reports were relayed back to the city.

The *Robert E. Lee* arrived in St. Louis on July 4 at 11:30 A.M., three days, eighteen hours, and fourteen minutes after departing New Orleans. Church bells rang out and cannon were shot. The *Natchez* arrived six hours and thirty-six minutes later. The two captains were wined and dined like royalty, but the *Robert E. Lee* had won the gilded horns in history's "Greatest Steamboat Race of All."

Despite her loss, the *Natchez* made 401 trips to and from New Orleans in the nine and a half years she was in service. Today the *Natchez IX,* one of only six steamboats on the Mississippi River, still sails out of New Orleans and regularly races against competitors to claim the golden horns.

DEGAS MISSES HIS TRAIN

- 1872 -

THE YOUNG MAN STEPPED OFF THE STEAMER AND WAS suddenly struck by the brightness of the sunlight filtering through the hot, humid air. He shielded his eyes with his hand to see better and then stared in wonderment at all the people who had turned out to meet him. They waved to him at first and then began shaking hands and hugging him. They were his family, a mix of brothers and sister-in-laws, uncles, nieces, and nephews. He felt as if he were on familiar territory, as if he were coming home.

He was glad to have finally arrived on solid ground. He could only describe the boat trip on the English paddle steamer, *Scotia,* from Liverpool to New York as interminably boring, especially as he spoke no English. But at least the trip had allowed him the chance to fill a notebook full of penciled sketches and caricatures of fellow passengers that he could later use in his artwork. The trip from New York City to New Orleans had been four tedious days spent in longing anticipation. When he arrived at the train depot on Lake

Pontchartrain, he was ecstatic to be reunited with his adoring New Orleans family. He stepped down off the train and felt immediately connected to the city of his mother's homeland. He was especially impressed that the Crescent City, one of the largest cities in America, was hailed as a prominent center for the arts. When he left Paris, the young man had been just beginning to establish himself as a painter. His short stay in New Orleans would provide the impetus to push him to the forefront of art world.

Edgar Degas was eager to meet everyone, but the sunlight was unbearable and the humidity even in October was stifling. He squinted his eyes and looked for a shady place to wait while everyone made the necessary preparations to head back toward the city.

The Degas family home at 2306 Esplanade Avenue sat on the edge of the busy French Quarter. It was a vibrant French mansion with a prominent double gallery from which one could look out over the city. The neighborhood was full of colorful personalities, characters that would live forever in Degas's paintings. His letters back to Paris spoke of his excitement with the novelties and sights of the city as he submerged himself in the unique Creole culture, discussed the heated political issues of the day, visited lavish plantation homes of family friends, and attended extravagant dinner parties thrown by the city's most elite citizens.

Eventually Degas fell into an easy daily routine. Much of his time was spent sketching and painting portraits of various family members. He was drawn to a particular melancholy young woman. Estelle, the widow of a nephew of Jefferson Davis, had married Degas's brother, Rene, and had borne him five children. Unfortunately, she was going blind. In his *Portrait of Estelle,* we see the woman arranging flowers with an exaggerated sense of touch. Degas sympathized with Estelle and her affliction as he had been experiencing eye troubles himself for a couple of years. The strong southern sun of New Orleans continued to bother his eyes and turned him indoors. Degas focused better in dark interiors and concentrated on close-up, intense subjects. He juxtaposed black skin against white and white cotton against black business attire. It was during his stay in New Orleans that Degas began to develop certain compositional effects, hand and head movements, arrangement of bodies—techniques that would reappear later in his famous ballet paintings. His bedroom served both as living quarters and studio.

After two months in post-Civil War New Orleans, amid various scandals and tragedies of the Reconstruction period, strained race relations, and family infidelities, Degas was ready to head back to Paris. He had painted more portraits than he cared to think about and his early excitement of visiting America's most exotic city had begun to wane. Temperatures were too hot, the sun was too strong, and his relatives were too demanding of his time.

He complained about trying to paint portraits of relatives, saying, "Nothing is as difficult as doing family portraits. To make a cousin sit for you and feeding an imp of two months is quite hard work."

His painting *Children on a Doorstep* displays this frustration, as does *Yard of a House (New Orleans),* which depicts children at play in the back of the house on Esplanade Avenue in a way that gives the impression that the children are not finished, but rather in the process of growing up. It was his work with fidgety children and restless relations that seems to have paved the way for Degas's impressionistic style of loose structure and unconfined compositions.

Woman Seated on a Balcony shows Mathilde Musson looking directly at the viewer, and the painting's asymmetrical composition was another technique perfected by Degas during his stay in New Orleans.

But Degas was eager to get to Paris and continue his life there. His bags packed, he was looking forward to an early January 1873 departure. The hands of fate, however, were spinning another story. Degas missed his train from New Orleans to New York, and consequently the steamer to Paris sailed without the artist on board. Degas had to console himself with a later sailing date on a French ship via Havana, Cuba.

It was during the next two months, before he sailed in March, that Degas began to visit the factory offices of Musson, Prestidge & Company, Cotton Factors and Commissioner Merchants, at 63 Carondelet Street (today it is at 407 Carondelet Street) on the corner of Perdido Street, owned and operated by family members. Intricately involved in war activities, his uncle and a group of cotton brokers had devised to withhold their produce from New Orleans in order to encourage French intervention in the Civil War. As punishment for this disobedience, the firm had been taxed $500 by the northern occupation force to help relieve the city's starving populace. After the war, the cotton business declined and the firm found itself on the brink of bankruptcy, desperately trying to make ends meet. Degas's seminal painting focuses on the bustling activities of fifteen individuals at work in the cotton offices. His uncle, senior partner of the firm, is featured in the painting, as well as his brother Rene, who nonchalantly reads the newspaper in the forefront. Brother Achille is portrayed as a dandy standing on the extreme left. *A Cotton Office in New Orleans* became the first impressionist painting bought by a French museum. Had Degas left on time as scheduled, this masterpiece would never have been painted. One year later Degas and his artist colleagues organized the first impressionist show in Paris.

Degas's stay in New Orleans was a turning point in his life and career. His intimate relationships with his New Orleans family and his experiences in a war-torn and defeated South engendered a new artistic freedom. Forced to stay indoors, he pioneered a new form of expression, and the impressionist movement, an era that would rock the art world, was born.

It is surprising that Degas was the only French impressionist to travel and work in America, and his New Orleans visit was a major milestone in his career. Christopher Benfry, Degas scholar, explains the impact of New Orleans on the artistry of the painter: "Degas was relatively obscure before his New Orleans sojourn . . . and hadn't yet settled on the subjects and styles that would occupy him during the following decades. He was a painter in transition, searching for his true self. And something about the city of New Orleans, itself in a period of rapid change, helped him focus his energies."

Degas referred to himself as "almost a son of Louisiana." He took all his New Orleans paintings and portraits of relatives with him back to Paris and held on to all but one of them until his death.

THE SPIRIT OF THE SULTAN'S PALACE

- 1873 -

The four-story mansion on the corner of Dauphiné Street and Orleans Avenue was built by the La Prete family in 1836. But after the Civil War, like many southern families who found themselves in dire straits with little ready cash, Jean Baptiste Le Prete was looking to rent out his spacious home. He planned to retire to his family's plantation home in Plaquemines Parish, miles away from the mosquito-infested city and its yellow-fever victims.

One evening he was approached by a man identifying himself as an emissary of a Turkish sultan. The man wanted a place for his brother and his entourage. Le Prete was delighted that a royal family, rather than a Yankee, would be taking up residence in his home and paying him for the privilege of doing so.

The residence, though large, was an ordinary house by all accounts. Delicate wrought-iron lace decorated the balconies, and a small courtyard and garden in the back offered respite from the intense heat. In the heart of the French Quarter, it was in a quiet neighborhood, blocks away from the debauchery of Bourbon Street.

The sultan arrived with his retinue of wives, children, harem girls, slaves, and muscular eunuchs and almost immediately began transforming Le Prete's mansion. He went to great lengths to shield the house from curious eyes of passersby. Heavy drapes were put on windows and iron bars were installed on locked doors and windows. He erected huge iron gates and locked them with heavy padlocks. Scimitar-armed men patrolled the balconies day and night.

Expensive and opulent furnishings were brought into the house, and some say it was as extravagant as any Turkish palace. Many believed the Turkish sultan had fled his homeland under peculiar circumstances, taking much of his wealth—piles of gold, jewelry, and other lavish treasures—with him. But whether he was an actual sultan or the brother of a sultan remained a question. In any case the prince ended up in New Orleans.

All seemed fine for nearly two years. Neighbors did complain about loud music and raucous laughter that lasted late into the night, but times were tough and most New Orleans families, hard hit by the ravages of the Civil War, were willing to overlook a little discomfort to help out their neighbors. Neighbors also described a smell of incense when the doors opened enough to allow someone in or out. Strange tinkling sounds emanated from the dark, ominous place, and stories circulated of opium-smoking orgies and sexual perversions.

The sultan was reported to be a cruel man. Some say he tortured his wives and slaves into submission; others even accused him of taking captives from the streets of New Orleans.

The eventual demise of the sultan's reign was first discovered by a neighbor passing in front of the house one morning. The sultan's palace was eerily silent, no laughter, no music. Even stranger was that the front gates were opened and the guards were nowhere to be seen.

As she stood on the corner, transfixed by the quietness, the neighbor noticed blood dripping from the edge of an upstairs gallery. Looking around she saw more blood cascading down the front steps as if the life was literally draining out of the house.

She immediately contacted the authorities, who, using a battering ram, broke through the front door.

The carnage inside stopped the officers short. Those who ventured forth found it hard to walk on the slippery, slick, blood-coated floor. Blood and body parts were strewn everywhere. Axes had been used as weapons to decapitate harem girls and mutilate slaves. The police reported that the bodies of the murdered men and women had "been raped and sexually mutilated in grotesque ways." A scene resembling a butcher shop showed every member of the household was dead, chopped to pieces. As it was impossible to say who was who and what body parts were whose, the victims would never be identified. Before the police left they went out into the courtyard, where one officer spotted a glove on the ground and moved in closer to see what evidence had been left at the scene. What he found was not a glove at all, but a hand reaching out from a newly dug pit. Here in a shallow grave lay the prince. There was so much dirt in his throat and esophagus that it was evident he had been buried alive. In a hellish ordeal, choking on soil and clay, he had tried desperately to claw his way out of the grave.

No one in the neighborhood had heard a sound throughout the bloodied night, and the extent of the horrible details was never revealed by the authorities.

A mysterious ship had docked along the Mississippi River, staying in port for only a day. Some say pirates had learned of the sultan's treasure and planned to steal the booty. But those who were acquainted with pirates say this could not be the case. First of all, pirates use pistols as their weapons of choice, and secondly, the people inside the house, white, black, woman, child, or eunuch, would have been much more valuable to pirates as live prisoners to be sold in the Caribbean slave market than as corpses.

What is more plausible is a grotesque tale of royal fratricide. During this time in Turkey, newly named sultans often feared threats to their power and that of their heirs from other branches of the family. To eliminate this fear, they would either imprison their brothers, called "princes," forever or kill them. Our prince had supposedly fled to New Orleans to hide from executioners. But he was discovered by the well-trained assassins, and when the prince's body was found, it was dressed in traditional Muslim funeral attire.

No one was ever charged with the murders. No one claimed the bodies.

But that is not the end of the story. Two women who lived in the house during separate times reported seeing the sultan's ghost. One moved out after hearing shrieks and gurgling sounds. Another owner told of nightly visits from the turbaned sultan and awakening to an eerie presence standing over her. Other residents of the house have complained of noises at night that sound like bodies hitting wooden floors. Neighbors swear they have seen the long, trailing silk robe of the sultan as he flits around the house. Some report apparitions of headless bodies oozing droplets of blood. The last person living at the house was said to have made friends with the prince, engaging his ghost in casual conversations. Today people report strange tinkling music and screams coming from the house late at night and the smell of incense around the house. A twisted tree has grown from the site where the sultan's body was buried in the courtyard.

This unsolved mystery remains the bloodiest crime and largest mass murder ever committed in New Orleans.

RINGING IN PROSPERITY

- 1884 -

City fathers hoped that hosting the World's Industrial and Cotton Centennial Exposition in war-ravaged New Orleans would signal a new beginning for the Crescent City and a new phase of North–South cooperation.

The Cotton Planters Association had suggested the exhibition to celebrate a hundred years of exporting cotton, and it was authorized by an Act of Congress on February 10, 1883. Mayor Joseph Valsin Guillotte and his delegation had many new ideas to bolster the city's economy and invigorate the 247 acres of Carrollton Park grounds that would be transformed into a world-class exhibition site.

Opening day, December 16, 1884, arrived at last, though it was nearly two weeks late due to bad weather and construction problems. But the city had readied itself for a full year of festivities and everyone had looked forward to finally getting things under way.

Celebration and fanfare was the order of the day despite the continuation of gloomy weather. Visitors thronging the streets had used many different means of transportation to get to the exposition. Some traveled a few miles by horse and buggy; others covered long distances by railroad or steamboat down the Mississippi River. The Main Building, housing the vast Music Hall, was a huge structure covering 33 acres with 23-foot-wide galleries that ran around the outside of the building. It was the largest building in the country at this time and held machinery that occupied more than 400,000 square feet. The entire area was abuzz with visitors ready to view the wonders of the world in action.

The morning began with the arrival of steamer guests at the exhibition wharf. A procession escorted by fair President Edmund Richardson marched its way to the Music Hall, patriotically decorated with flags of all sizes. Officers of the Washington Artillery in elegantly detailed uniforms proudly rode ahead, leading the parade of rank and file military men. They sounded the opening shots of the exposition while the Excelsior Brass band led the opening march.

In his introductory speech Richardson presented the exposition to U.S. President Chester A. Arthur, one of the exposition's early supporters. From his executive mansion in Washington, D.C., Arthur opened the event with a telegraph address and, via electric current, set into motion the great Harris–Corliss engines that provided the 6,000 horsepower needed to run the exposition's machinery.

The centennial was a grand affair. It boasted more than 5,000 incandescent lights, 75,000 exhibitors, an average daily attendance of 7,500 visitors, and a Refrigeration and Cold Storage House that produced five tons of ice per day.

Sightseers at the fair could ride the Electric Railroad, a 3-mile track that circled the exposition grounds every few minutes, and indulge a sweet tooth with a soda for 10 cents a glass. The Brazilian exhibit provided samples of 624 different types of coffee, and the Horticulture Hall introduced the water hyacinth to the United States.

Visitors hoped to see some of the prominent persons who graced the fairgrounds. John Philip Sousa played at the exposition. Thomas Lipton of Lipton Iced Teas was among the distinguished guests, as was writer Grace King. Julia Ward Howe presided over the Woman's Exhibition. Fairgoers were entertained and often stunned by Buffalo Bill and his Wild West Show. More than fifty Indians rode through the streets, open air demonstrations showed off shooting skills, and extravaganza animal acts included donkeys, elk, and Texas steer.

To make the exposition even more special, Mayor Guillotte had a unique idea. He directed Exposition Special Commissioner S. Prentiss Nutt to write to the mayor of Philadelphia, William B. Smith, asking that the Liberty Bell be sent to New Orleans. His words were inspirational, "Our ancestors fought and bled for the time-enduring principles which that bell rang out on July 4, 1776 . . . are we not co-inheritors of its glories?" Citizens of New Orleans signed the petition asking that the symbolic bell of freedom be sent to their city. Mayor Smith made his case for sending the bell to New Orleans to the Select and Common Councils of Philadelphia, saying: ". . . the presence of the Old Bell . . . can . . . make evident to the people of the South that the City of Brotherly Love . . . is anxious to aid in the restoration of perfect harmony throughout the nation."

The councils voted in favor of sending the bell provided that three policemen accompany and watch over it at all times.

On January 23, 1885, the Liberty Bell was ceremoniously removed from Independence Hall and began its trip south. Suspended on a metal frame secured to a flat railcar, the bell could be clearly seen by the crowds along the tracks. Throughout the countryside people cheered its passing, bells rang out, ceremonies were held, and cannon were fired everywhere the Liberty Bell stopped. After fourteen stops, the Liberty Bell arrived in New Orleans and was displayed in the Main Building under the banner: 1776 PROCLAIM

LIBERTY. A miniature, cast-iron Liberty Bell became a popular souvenir item at the fair.

A month later the soulful strains of T. V. Baquet, veteran cornet player, led his Excelsior Cornet Band to open the Colored People's Exhibit in the Main Building. The *Daily Picayune* recognized "the well-known Excelsior Cornet Band of this city," which accompanied Straight University Glee Club's program. Many of the city's prominent leaders spoke, including P. B. S. Pinchback, the first black acting governor of the state of Louisiana from 1872 to 1873.

The exposition was a success in many respects, but not financially. More than six million people attended the exposition, which stimulated tremendous growth in the Carrollton area, where today many fine and elegant homes can be found. One of its only remaining cast-iron gates is part of Hebrew Rest Cemetery. Rex, king of Mardi Gras, minted its first doubloon that season to celebrate the fair. All U.S. states and territories, except Utah, and more than twenty foreign countries participated in the exhibits and displays. It was the largest U.S. World Exposition to date.

BLACK INDIANS PARADE THROUGH TOWN

- 1885 -

The winter had been dreary with rain and cold temperatures. Christmas and New Year's had come and gone as New Orleanians turned their attention on the upcoming carnival season, sewing costumes, collecting "throws," and designing themes for masquerade balls and pageants.

Mardi Gras Day, February 17, 1885, was the last in a long string of festivities that had started on January 6, the Feast of the Epiphany or Twelfth Night. There were a lot of visitors in the city, many of whom had come in December to see the World's Industrial and Cotton Centennial Exposition, celebrating a century of the United States exporting cotton, then stayed to participate in the nation's biggest party. Even Buffalo Bill and his traveling Wild West troupe would participate in Mardi Gras parades.

The celebrations had been gathering momentum, and revelers woke early on Fat Tuesday imbued with the *joie de vivre* of the season.

Busy with the final preparations for the grandest day of all, men, women, and children wiggled into costumes from the simple to the extravagant. They would take to the streets dressed as milkmaids, witches, clowns, Spanish girls, buccaneers, or any other number of personas. Families would pack hefty lunches because this would be an all-day event. For persons of color in the city, Mardi Gras Day itself was even more special: It was the only day of the year that they were allowed to wear costumes or hide behind masks. When the clock struck midnight, all rowdiness and revelry would end, and the Lenten season would begin.

Mardi Gras was a celebration of freedom and a time to be arrogant and disobedient. While white and Creole citizens lined Canal Street, St. Charles Avenue, and the narrow streets of the French Quarter to see the Rex and Proteus parades, black neighborhoods had their own way of celebrating Mardi Gras. The 1885 Rex Krewe invitation to its extravagant ball was a die-cut promotional piece showing various scenes of chivalry as its theme. But former slaves or free persons of color, repressed and oppressed, would not be witness to any show of chivalry. Revolting against widespread exclusion from Mardi Gras celebrations, blacks began their own carnival traditions. Some groups held balls in secluded locations; others paraded through black neighborhoods in a risky show of artistic expression. Many took the opportunity to act mischievous for a day, masquerading behind masks and costumes.

New Orleans blacks, usually isolated from outside influences, had found themselves exposed to new ideas and peoples brought to the city by the Cotton Exposition. They had watched the visiting Plains Indians perform dances and hold shooting contests in Buffalo Bill's Pony Express demonstrations and Deadwood stagecoach acts, held in the popular black recreation area called the Oakland Park and Riding Stables. Free men of color, still struggling for the equality and civil rights that had been promised to them nearly twenty years before by Lincoln's Emancipation Proclamation, found inspiration and hope in the free, expressive, and self-assured Indians they saw entertaining huge crowds at the stables.

This Mardi Gras the city seemed alive with a new boldness. Carnival-goers lined the streets to see the sights and sounds of the vivid costumes and noisy merrymakers. Suddenly they were caught off guard with the appearance of the city's black denizens parading openly in stunning full Indian regalia. Though most had gotten used to seeing the Indians of Buffalo Bill's Wild West Show roaming the streets in native garb, most were shocked by the spectacle of black Indians parading for the first time!

The colorful marching club, called the Creole Wild West, was led by Big Chief Becate Batiste, a New Orleans free black man of African, French, and Choctaw descent, who felt an affinity with the Indian and wanted to honor him. The costumed men of the "tribe" wore brightly colored hand-sewn Indian garb inlaid with intricate beadwork. Magnificent headdresses were uniquely designed using feathers, a mainstay of West African masking traditions.

The unique pageantry of the black Indians started in the ancestral neighborhoods of the city's Seventh Ward, in quarters called La Nouvelle Marigny, an area roughly bordered by St. Claude, St. Bernard, and Elysian Fields Avenues. Marchers strutted past the small Creole cottages and shotgun houses and ventured out and about the city. They had no publicized route, no parade permit.

Well before they could be seen, the black Indians could be heard chanting and singing in a call and response traditional oral style that many could trace back to their Haitian and West African origins. *"T'ouwais, bas q'ouwais,"* one Indian would call out, throwing his head back and downward.

He would be answered by members of the tribe, *"Ou tendais."*

Farther down their marching route, amid bending knees and rhythmic swaying, mysterious words and Creole patois, "Tu-way-pa-ka-way, tu-way-pa-ka-way," filled the streets. "Ungai-ah! Ungai-ha!" cried other braves on parade. Carrying tomahawks and spears, the Indians sang and danced the Congo Square Bamboula to the beat of drums and tambourines. Some shook cowbells and rattles as they second-lined to the changa beat. Marching and chanting in Indian costumes had irrevocably been established as a replacement for the banned practices of Congo Square dancing and voodoo rituals.

Black men, bolstered by the victory of getting the first exhibit of African-American history on display at the Cotton Exposition, identified a shared vision of freedom with the Indians who had once provided refuge to runaway slaves. By masking as Indians, these men stepped forward to participate as never before in the city's premier celebration, Mardi Gras. The vibrant black Indians stunned carnival participants and started a lasting tradition—and that's what Mardi Gras is all about.

Jazz greats Jelly Roll Morton and Louis Armstrong claimed to have been influenced by the black Indian music they heard practiced in the streets of New Orleans as children. Today the New Orleans Mardi Gras Indian Council helps preserve and enrich the Indian culture. Thirty-five "tribes" parade in elaborate Indian costumes and headdresses, each weighing more than 200 pounds and costing thousands of dollars. They are among the most exquisite and colorful sights of Mardi Gras in New Orleans.

ITALY DEMANDS RETRIBUTION

- 1891 -

David C. Hennessy joined the New Orleans police force as a young man to support his widowed mother. After much hard work and dedication, he was appointed to the position of police chief, by Mayor Joseph Shakspeare after the election of 1888. He was known as an honest, hard-working lawman.

New Orleans, like much of the rest of the country, was in the tightening jaws of an economic depression in the late nineteenth century. Racial tension and anti-immigrant sentiment were rampant in the Crescent City, especially against the Sicilians who were arriving in great numbers and competing with the locals for the few available jobs. Their dark, Sicilian complexion and possible gangster connections were seen as basis enough for blatant discrimination by other nationalities. Many Italians had been brought to Louisiana by sugar and cotton planters to work the crops, but they seemed to prefer the city and came to dominate the fruit, oyster, and fish trades. They settled mostly in the French Quarter.

Hennessy took his job as police chief seriously and worked tirelessly to uncover illegal mob activities in the city. He eventually gained national recognition for his capture of Sicilian Giuseppe Esposito, a known Mafia bigwig. Racial tensions were growing, and an area of increased lawlessness on Decatur Street in the French Quarter was nicknamed "Vendetta Alley." Hennessy set to ordering the arrests of the men he believed to be responsible for organized crime.

But Hennessy was being watched carefully by those he was accusing. On a cool, rainy evening, October 15, 1890, he was ambushed at 11:25 P.M. on Basin Street near his Girod Street home. He was returning from a police board meeting when a group of men with sawed-off shotguns fired at him from a run-down house across the street. He fired back, but receiving six shots, he collapsed.

Mayor Shakspeare, a well-liked and capable politician, blamed Sicilian gangsters for Hennessy's death. He arrested more than a hundred suspects. The business community was enraged by the killing of the police chief and formed a well-financed paralegal organization called the "Committee of Fifty" to help convict the assassins. The group included public officials, lawyers, newspapermen, bankers, and businessmen.

In the end, nineteen Italians were indicted for Hennessy's murder, and the first nine were to be tried in February 1891. Jury selection took twelve days. One of the gunmen's confessions was never admitted as evidence, and several key witnesses were never called to testify, but most believed the case against the assassins was strong.

The Italians in the city, however, felt the men had been wrongly accused and were being used as scapegoats because of the hatred many felt toward the Sicilians. New Orleans Italians urged their fellow countrymen across the nation to contribute to their defense fund. Money poured in, and a team of five top trial lawyers was hired.

Some felt the Italians got the best legal counsel because of ill-gained money and suspect connections.

Italian–Americans waited nervously to hear the fate of their brothers. The rest of the city waited for revenge.

The city was in shock on March 13 when six of the nine indicted were found innocent, due to lack of evidence, and a mistrial was declared for the other three. Rumors of jury tampering, bribery, and intimidation surfaced. Facing further charges, the nine Italians were returned to Parish Prison.

Hot heads and retaliatory schemes were rampant. An editorial in a New Orleans newspaper challenged the citizenry: "Rise, outraged people of New Orleans! Let those who have attempted to sap the very foundation of your Temples of Justice be in one vengeful hour swept from your midst. Peaceably if you can, forcibly if you must!"

A speaker incited a meeting of enraged locals with the words: "When courts fail, the people must act. What protection is there left us when the very head of our police department, our chief of police, is assassinated in our very midst and his assassins are turned loose on the community?"

A vigilante committee placed an ad in the local paper calling for supporters to attend a meeting and to "come prepared for action."

Thousands of people responded to the ad and met at the Henry Clay statue on Canal Street. Rabble-rousers calling for justice and vindication incited the crowd to do what the courts had failed to do.

When word of the plan got out, the mayor, hidden away in the Pickwick Club and unofficially supportive of the crowd, was not available to stop the impending action. When news reached the capital, Governor Francis Nicholls said he could do nothing without the mayor's request.

March 14, 1891, dawned bright and sunny, a day full of promise that would end black and ugly. By 10:00 A.M. a crowd of thousands had gathered in the streets.

The mob of 6,000 to 8,000 angry citizens, including many prominent people, marched to the city armory, where they armed themselves with weapons. Feeling powerful and vengeful, they proceeded to the Old Parish Prison on Bienville Street.

Battering rams were used to break into the jail. In the prison yard the armed men opened fire on a group of Italians huddled together. Only 20 feet away, their aim did not have to be careful to be lethal. They fired over a hundred shots from rifles and shotguns into the six helpless men, blasting their bodies apart. Others were hunted down in their cells and executed. Several of the corpses were dragged out into the streets and hung on lampposts for the mob to see. The cheers of the crowd were nearly deafening.

In the end, eleven men who had not been found guilty of anything were dead.

Italians worldwide were outraged, but many U.S. newspapers approved the action. A grand jury laid the blame on the raging mob of people; but not only were the vigilantes never brought to justice, they in fact became local heroes.

An unlikely participant in this saga was lifting her indignant head across the ocean. The Italian government was outraged at the mob killing. Three of the men were Italian citizens. Italy brought immediate action against the city through its foreign minister, who took the matter before the U.S. State Department. Italy removed its minister from Washington, D.C., and this led to the subsequent withdrawal of the American ambassador from Rome.

This was a serious predicament. There was soon talk of war, and it was reported that Italian warships were streaming towards the United States. President Benjamin Harrison sprang into action and publicly denounced the lynchings. The United States ultimately paid the Italian government $25,000 as retribution for the deaths of its citizens.

Anti-immigrant sentiment continued in the city, however, until the 1920s, when the U.S. Congress enacted severe restrictions on immigration and the great era of Italian immigration was halted. The mob action of 1891 resulted in the largest mass lynching in U.S. history.

Hennessy is buried in a Metairie Cemetery vault. A massive column of granite adorned with a symbolic replica of the chief's police belt and club marks the spot. The New Orleans Police Department's star-and-crescent badge lies near the base of his gravesite.

THE FIGHT OF THE CENTURY

- 1892 -

Boxing flourished in New Orleans despite the nation's rejection of bare-knuckled violence. But by 1892, even this street-brawling city had entered a new age of legitimate prizefighting. The Fistic Carnival was meant to celebrate the new pugilism, a boxing style that would rely more on skill and science than brawn.

By Thursday evening, September 7, 1892, thousands of prizefighting enthusiasts had witnessed two extraordinary matches. Lightweight champion Jack MacAuliffe had retained his title by knocking out Billy Meyer on the first day of competition, and the next day featherweight champion George Dixon had knocked out Jack Skelly in the eighth round.

Now on the final night of the Fistic Carnival, attendees eagerly awaited the main event—the match between John L. Sullivan, heavyweight champion of the world, and Jim Corbett, contender.

The four-story Olympic Club took up the entire block bounded by Chartres and Royal Streets and was festooned with banners hanging from its roof. Electric lights spit with uncontrolled energy in every window of the athletic club. Streetcars arrived, one after the other, delivering nearly 10,000 excited spectators, the largest number ever to attend a fight. Special Pullman train cars arrived from Buffalo and Chicago. The upcoming presidential election and the deadly cholera epidemic were shoved off the front pages of the nation's newspapers. Tickets went for $5.00 to $15.00.

Inside the arena, telegraphs clattered loudly sending reports to New York City's Pulitzer building, where bulletins announcing round-by-round reports interrupted regular programming. Promptly at 9:00 P.M. John Duffy, referee of the event, stepped into the heavily roped ring. The audience exploded in an ovation that recognized Duffy's stature as an honest and skillful referee. Famed Bat Masterson would serve as timekeeper for the match.

Sullivan, the heavyweight titleholder, was a legend. With a volatile temperament he had scraped his way to the top of the boxing world using raw power and the tenacity of a working-class tough guy. He captured the nation's attention when he hopped on a stage in Boston and hastily roughed up a local challenger. He pummeled opponents whenever he could, and when he knocked out Patrick "Paddy" Ryan in 1882, he earned the title Bare-Knuckle Heavyweight-Boxing Champion of the World. He held his title for decades, defending it over thirty times.

"Gentleman Jim" Corbett epitomized the new era. He had earned his reputation from his highbrow, dapper manner and use of scientific technique in the fighting clubs on the West Coast. An educated man who had been a bank clerk, he spent time before a fight analyzing an opponent's strengths and weaknesses. Then with a deft combination of speed and style in the ring, he would defeat his enemy.

In 1890 New Orleans had legalized boxing under the Marquis of Queensbury Rules, which called for padded gloves, three-minute rounds, and a one-minute rest between rounds for fighters, all staged in a roped-in 24-foot-square area. Tonight, under these rules, gloved participants would contend for the heavyweight title.

Tension was high. In one corner stood Sullivan, thirty-three, the four-to-one favorite (although some gave odds as high as seven to one), weighing in at 212 pounds. MacAuliffe, who had just secured his lightweight title two days earlier, was there to offer advice.

The other corner held twenty-six-year-old Corbett, the challenger, at 187 pounds. With him was Mike Donovan, a renowned boxing technician who had previously fought Sullivan. He would give advice about style and tactics.

The fight started with Sullivan rushing at Corbett in his bullying style of boxing. He was a powerful hitter, with exceptional strength in his right arm. Corbett remained cool, easily sidestepping Sullivan's "fast and first" attacks. But fans worried that Corbett could not avoid the powerful jabs for long.

The arena was packed with spectators. Some simply enjoyed the thrill of the sport; many had huge sums of money riding on the outcome.

In the third round Corbett landed a weighty left and broke Sullivan's nose. Blood splattered everywhere and continued to flow throughout the fight. But Sullivan was known for his toughness and the punishment he could take. Fans yelled for more.

By the seventh round, Corbett was in control. He attacked Sullivan's body, burying lefts and rights into the champion. Corbett was boxing flawlessly as he danced around the ring. Sullivan's temper flared in the face of defeat. He punched furiously in the brawling style that had brought him so much success, but his attempts were easily sidestepped by the bobbing and weaving Corbett.

Jeers from spectators urged Sullivan to attack the challenger. But by the fourteenth round it was obvious that Sullivan's style of boxing would not prevail. Corbett was landing blow after blow and Sullivan had little energy to retaliate. By the twenty-first round, Sullivan was exhausted; he staggered under Corbett's battery of punches and grabbed hold of the ring rope. A Corbett right dropped Sullivan to his knees and a final left-right combination flattened the champion to the mat.

Referee Duffy began the count when the once immortal Sullivan went down and declared victory for Corbett as the new heavyweight champion. The crowd exploded. In the heady thrill of the night, audience members threw pieces of their clothing into the ring—belts, hats, canes. Flowers from suit lapels were strewn across the ring. A spectator likened the scene to "a whole herd of Kansas cyclones." A new era of boxing had begun, one that would limit violence in the ring and at the same time usher in a new enthusiasm for the sport nationwide.

Duffy silenced the crowd as Sullivan staggered to address his boxing fans. He said, "All I have to say is that I came into the ring once too often—and if I had to get licked I'm glad I was licked by an American. I remain your warm and personal friend, John L. Sullivan."

In the "Fight of the Century" Corbett had accomplished the unthinkable task of beating the legendary Sullivan, who admitted to losing his shirt in the fight, betting on himself. He added, "Thousands of my friends all over the country, who thought I was unbeatable, I guess, lost their shirts, too. That is the thing that makes me so sore about this fight."

During his lengthy career, Sullivan fought thirty-seven matches, totaling thirty-two wins, one loss, three draws, and one no-decision. He was inducted into the Boxing Hall of Fame in 1954.

Corbett capitalized on his defeat of Sullivan. He left boxing after he subsequently lost his championship title, and went on the Broadway stage. He also acted in one of Thomas Edison's early films. He had only nineteen professional fights, won eleven, lost four, and had two draws and two no-contests.

New Orleans was the stage for many boxing contests in early fight history. Another notable battle was the 110-round contention in 1893 between Andy Bowen and Jack Burke, which lasted seven hours and nineteen minutes, going into the record books as the longest boxing match under Queensbury rules. The contest ended in a no-decision, as both men were exhausted and unable to continue the fight. The Olympic Club, once called "the cradle of American boxing," burned to the ground early in the nineteenth century and was not rebuilt.

THE SILVER SCREEN FINDS A HOME

- 1896 -

At the end of the nineteenth century, New Orleanians were enjoying diverse Sunday pleasures. Coffee drinkers gathered in Exchange Alley coffeehouses to catch up on the latest news. Distinguished gentlemen socialized and sipped Southern Comfort served directly from whiskey barrels on Bourbon Street. Couples strolled arm in arm along the Mississippi levee after church services. Black, white, yellow, and brown music lovers danced and swooned to the beat of the ragtime tunes that had become the rage. But a new form of entertainment, one that would revolutionize the country, was about to be born in the Crescent City.

Walter Wainwright and William T. Rock, despite the menacing heat wave, were more anxious than hot on Sunday, July 26, 1896, as they stood on the corner of Exchange Place and Canal Street staring up at their theater's new sign, Vitascope Hall.

Rock was a colorful, rotund Englishman who wore an impressive gold watch and chain across his chest. "Pop" Rock, as he was called around town, had been very successful with peep-show boxes that made still pictures dance in the one-viewer machines. But there was more advanced technology on the horizon—new moving pictures. He paid $1,500 to secure the Louisiana rights of the patented Vitascope projector from the inventor, Thomas A. Edison, himself.

Wainwright had been a carnival tightrope walker, known as Wainretta. He was looking forward to making his fortune in the new industry and had risked his circus career and financial security to do so.

The two partners scoured the street searching for paying customers. They had spent a considerable sum of money to outfit Vitascope Hall. The large first-floor room was packed with 400 seats of crowded benches and folding chairs bought from a bankrupt funeral parlor. They had hung great sheets of black canvas over the windows to keep out the intense, penetrating summer light. A large white fabric was stretched tight across a frame mounted at the front of the room. Needing an experienced man to work the new moving-picture Vitascope machine, they hired William A. Reed, a projectionist from Koster and Bial's live performance music hall.

At first the trio arranged for outdoor viewings of their films to accompany the band performances at West End, a popular amusement park and resort on Lake Pontchartrain. When it was time for the motion pictures to be shown, a curtain would be stretched across the bandstand. At a fair in Gentilly, an open plain north of the city, Rock set up a huge white canvas screen and paid a local engineer, Allen B. Blakemore, to run an electricity line from a nearby overhead-powered streetcar line to his Vitascope machine. Though the outdoor venues were not ideal, New Orleans audiences were exposed to the incredible moving pictures. A month later, the Vitascope Hall advertised its first indoor theater showing. But Wainwright and Rock worried whether people would pay to see just films, without live acts or bands.

By 10:00 A.M. crowds had congregated under the Vitascope Hall sign with the dime admission held tightly in their sweating fists. It seems the magic of moving pictures had captured the imagination of New Orleanians. Music halls in the north had already experimented with showing films by playing them along with live performances. News reports had championed their innovation. The Vitascope Hall had gone one step further; it would be the country's first permanent motion-picture theater, established solely for the purpose of showing moving pictures.

The paying public filed into the darkened hall. Some would sit elbow to elbow with fellow patrons; others would stand along the walls. All would be captivated by the whir of the Vitascope machine as it projected moving images onto the wide screen in the front of the darkened room. The first shows consisted of five short vignettes of various scenes such as Niagara Falls or Coney Island, a dance by the Devoe Sisters, or brief boxing or wrestling action. The films were shown continuously, over and over again. The first show ran from 10:00 A.M. to 3:00 P.M. The evening show went from 6:00 to 10:00 P.M.

The opening of Vitascope Hall was successful beyond belief. Rock and Wainwright brought in new films such as *The Record of a Sneeze, Sandow Flexing His Muscles, Boxing Cats, Pie Eating Contest,* or *Ella Lola's Turkish Dance* to replace those previously shown. The proprietors wanted to keep their paying public coming back again and again. And come back they did.

Crowds thronged to see William Heise's silent classic, *The Kiss.* Just 50 feet of film that ran twelve seconds, it was the most talked about film sequence of the time. In the film May Irwin and John C. Rice actually put their lips together. It was the medium's first kissing scene, and it created a furor both among those who couldn't see the scene enough and those who thought it was immoral to the core. In a letter to the editor of the *New Orleans Item,* a concerned citizen demanded the "too suggestive scene" be cut from the program. The editor would have none of the threat of censorship and responded that to find kissing to be immoral was "to open the eyes of the world to a flaw in something that they held to be without blemish."

The managers paid the criticism no heed as well and continued to show the short film to sold-out audiences. Moviegoers didn't even mind the jerky movements of the characters of early silent films. They fell in love with the movies and were intrigued with the advanced technology. Ever eager to make their fortunes, Wainwright and Rock offered their patrons a glimpse inside the projection booth for an additional dime. Those who chose to pay up could watch the man in the rear projection booth operate the great magical Vitascope machinery for a minute or so. For still another dime theatergoers could purchase a souvenir of their experience—a piece of unused film celluloid to call their very own.

Rock took out weekly ads and relied heavily on hyperbole to garner enthusiasm for Vitascope Hall. One ad proclaimed: "The Great Craze of the Day, Edison's Vitascope/New Series of Thrilling Views Photographic Motion at Last Perfected/The Dream of a Century Realized."

The Picayune participated in the hype, lauding the theater and reporting, "Here the Vitascope can be seen to better advantage than in the open air, where the winds and arc lights interfered with the rays of light thrown upon the screen."

Wainwright and Rock's Vitascope Hall, the first permanent theater in the entire country, extended its first run well beyond the expected summer season. By popular demand films were shown through September, but by October the Vitascope was touring the state, bringing the magic of moving pictures to small towns across Louisiana. The people of New Orleans would have to wait until the following spring, when the Vitascope would again come to a theater near them.

The passion for the new entertainment form was shared by many. In an August 19, 1896, letter sent to her sister in Baltimore, a New Orleans resident, Emma, wrote after attending a motion-picture show, "there is something magical about pictures in motion."

In the ensuing years, Wainwright disappeared from film industry records, but Reed was hailed as the king of motion-picture projectionists. Rock became an early movie industry mogul, serving as president of the Vitagraph Company of America, which eventually became the production arm of Warner Brothers. Vitascope Hall's place in film history was almost forgotten until British researcher Patrick Robertson stumbled across irrefutable evidence in the moldy records of the Society of Motion Pictures Engineers that proved Vitascope Hall was indeed the first permanent film theater in the country. Unfortunately, the unmarked site of Vitascope Hall is today a fast-food restaurant.

WORKING FOR THE VOTE

- 1903 -

The Athenaeum Hall on prestigious St. Charles Avenue had been the scene of many Mardi Gras balls, but on this sultry spring day, a somber Lenten atmosphere prevailed throughout the city. There was serious business to address. Men and women had sacrificed to make this day a reality. Some had worked for decades, and others had given their lives.

The 1,200 people assembled in the hall were the elite of the country. Physicians, teachers, businessmen, and political leaders, men and women, sat side by side, but many more wanted to get in. A crowd had gathered outside the auditorium straining to hear any news from inside.

The thirty-fifth annual convention of the National American Woman Suffrage Association (NAWSA) was called to order in the packed Athenaeum by its young president, the already quite famous Mrs. Carrie Chapman Catt. Audience members sat on the edges of their seats leaning forward, now anticipating the appearance of the most famous suffragist in the world.

Attending conventions such as this had become commonplace for the eighty-three-year-old icon seated on the stage. Though she often failed to realize her own importance, as honorary president of the organization she knew she would be called forth to take a bow. Young girls and middle-aged matrons stood in hushed respect as an aging Susan B. Anthony stepped forward to receive loving accolades and bouquets of Marechal Niel roses. The hall erupted in thunderous applause. The great woman was shocked by the sudden uproar that exploded in the hall and asked her escort what had happened. Anna Howard Shaw, destined to be president of the organization herself in a few years, explained that this ovation was for her, Susan B. Anthony.

Anthony, eighty-three, had been working for women's rights for four decades. She had stood before lecterns when audiences were small and accomplishments were negligible. She had seen the National Woman Suffrage Association merge with the American Woman Suffrage Association. She had been arrested and ridiculed. Anthony steadied herself and addressed the group. She spoke eloquently of her memorable visit to New Orleans for the World's Industrial and Cotton Centennial Exposition in 1884, and when she concluded, the audience clamored to its feet, cheering with excitement and waving handkerchiefs and fans.

Mrs. Catt, known for her persuasive acumen and powerful logic, then gave her opening address. A press notice of the event reported, "A distinguished Justice of the Supreme Court who was present remarked to the writer: 'I have heard many men, but not one can compare with Mrs. Catt in eloquence and logical power.'"

Mrs. Catt was also treated to an immediate standing ovation by the ebullient audience.

And so it was that in the city of New Orleans, sheltered by the ancient oaks of the Garden District, the Convention of 1903 bridged the two distinct periods of accomplishment in the suffrage movement.

Past met present. The first generation of suffragists who had labored long and hard to lay the foundation for legal rights converged with young, energetic new reformers. Anthony, who would pass away within three years, stood in stark contrast to Catt, who would go on to form the League of Women Voters and work for world peace for forty more years.

Other addresses were given by visitors and locals alike. Mrs. Emma S. Olds of Ohio spoke out on behalf of the Supreme Hive of the Ladies of the Maccabees, the largest business organization of women in the world. The Friday evening program opened with a prayer by the Reverend Gilbert Dobbs, which stirred the fighting spirit of the attendees: "While not often has the call been to women to don armor and press on to battle, yet it may well be that Thou hast reserved them for the battle of the ballots." These were fighting words, and convention attendees were battle-ready.

On Saturday evening the Reverend R. Wilkinson opened the session with his call: "God bless the women engaged in this work! God knows that if this city has in any way been lifted up, it has been through the efforts of noble women."

Dr. Cora Smith Eaton from Minnesota rallied, "O, men of the South, your savior is the southern woman! Put into her hand the ballot of full enfranchisement, like that you carry in your own hand on election day."

For Sunday services at 4:00 P.M. in the Athenaeum, the Reverend Anna Howard Shaw, a suffragist, gave a sermon directing women to "hold fast that which thou hast, that no man take thy crown."

News also reached those who wanted to read about the events. Speeches were covered by the *Woman's Journal,* the official paper of the National American Woman Suffrage Association. Founded in 1869 by Henry Blackwell and Alice Stone Blackwell, the paper had a weekly circulation of 4,500. The New Orleans *Daily Picayune* was replete with news coverage as well, describing convention audiences as "magnificent."

On Monday, M. J. Sanders, president of the Progressive Union of New Orleans, gave his enlightening address: "I believe my own state of mind on the woman suffrage question when I attended your first public meeting last Thursday evening represented fairly the average male opinion in this city—one of moderate ignorance and considerable indifference. Since listening to the addresses here I have had my ignorance largely dispelled and my indifferences dissipated, I hope forever."

One of the highlights of the conference was the now famous "The Woman with the Broom" speech given by Mrs. Elizabeth M. Gilmer of New Orleans: "My plea is for the domestic woman—the woman who is the mainstay of the world, who is back of every great enterprise and who makes possible the achievements of men—the woman behind the broom, who is the hardest-worked and worst-paid laborer on the face of the earth."

There were many ups and downs during the convention. One high was the unveiling of the new suffrage postage stamp, a college girl in cap and gown holding a tablet inscribed, "In Wyoming, Colorado, Utah and Idaho women vote on the same terms as men." Delegates hoped to embarrass other states into voting for women's rights. Then there was the exciting news that the Arizona Territory had given women the right to vote, but there was little time to celebrate: A second telegram followed that announced the governor had vetoed the bill.

Behind the convention's success were two New Orleans sisters, Kate Gordon, founder of the Era Club, which had hosted the convention, and Jean Gordon. Kate was given an inscribed loving cup; Jean held a bouquet of roses. The *Picayune* reported, "They tried to speak but their hearts were too full."

Convention-goers had a marvelous time in New Orleans. The Railway Company gave tours in special cars, taking visitors to Audubon Park, the Horticultural Hall, cemeteries, City Park, and antique shops. Others took boat trips on the Mississippi River to view sugar plantations.

During the longest suffrage convention ever held, every session was overcrowded. Ten glorious days gave renewed impetus to the women's suffrage movement, for it was here that the NAWSA voted to launch a new tactic to achieve universal suffrage. It was at the New Orleans convention of 1903 that delegates accepted a states' rights structure and, through a series of well-orchestrated state campaigns under Catt's guidance, secured the passage of the Nineteenth Amendment in 1920.

The Athenaeum on St. Charles Avenue, the site where history marched into the future, where inspired orators rocked the halls, and where ordinary men and women had stood up to be counted, burned down in 1905. The NAWSA evolved into the League of Women Voters and today focuses on educating women about the political process; the New Orleans chapter was formed in 1942.

LIKE A BIRD IN THE SKY

- 1910 -

It was New Year's Eve, December 31, 1910. Huge crowds had gathered in various venues throughout the city for the weeklong festivities of the New Orleans Aviation Tournament. Thousands had turned out at Lafayette Square to see John B. Moisant in his Aluminoplane spiraling upward into the sky and then plummeting downward toward the hard earth, pulling up at the last minute to come down again and then easing, brakeless, to a full rest.

At City Park spectators had watched some of the famous Moisant International Aviators, such as Roland Garros, billed as "The Cloud Kisser," and Rene Simon, whom the press had named "The Fool Flyer," attempt to break records for both altitude and duration. Also in town were Rene Barrier, "The Record Holder of Flights over Cities," and Edmund Audemars, nicknamed "Tiny" because his stature was small and because he piloted "the smallest and most dangerous aeroplane in the world." The flying daredevils captured the adventuresome spirit of the people watching safely from the ground.

The "birdmen" had arrived in New Orleans by train. But not just any train. This train was specially outfitted for the much touted "flying circus." It sported its own repair shop and carried a large tent and grandstands for spectators. More than ten roustabouts and as many ticket sellers and press agents traveled with the fearless flyers. Air exhibitions had become a serious moneymaking business. Also carted into town on the rails were the dozen or so airplanes needed for the exhibition, several mechanics, and numerous boxes of spare parts. The large tent was pitched on the New Orleans City Park racetrack, which had been closed to horse racing two years earlier. Box seats could cost upward of $1.50, while general admission was usually 50 cents. Anyone who was anyone turned out for the flying spectacles.

There had been some setbacks in the short history of flying. The Walter Wellman crash in October was still fresh in the public's mind, and the death of aviator Ralph Johnstone at an exhibition show in Denver a month later had stunned the nation. *Scientific American* had announced, "To affirm that the airplane is going to revolutionize the future is to be guilty of the wildest exaggeration." But progress was not to be stopped, and 1910 had certainly been a banner year for the burgeoning aviation industry. Everyone looked forward to records being broken at this International Aviation Tournament.

Earlier in the week French aviator Rene Simon had already set a record for flying a mile in 57 seconds and at a record height of 7,125 feet. Yesterday, December 30, in an extraordinary promotion pitting the airplane against the automobile, the 150-horsepower Packard consistently outraced the 50-horsepower Bleriot monoplane flown by Moisant, though only by a hair, in a 5-mile (8-kilometer) race.

Moisant was a thirty-seven-year-old French-Canadian pilot who had accumulated some renown barnstorming across the country with his "flying circus" of aviators. Independently wealthy, he was a bold and brash aviator who thrived on being in the spotlight. He had designed, produced, and flown the first experimental aluminum aircraft in 1909. Earlier this year, he had been the first to fly with a passenger onboard across the English Channel. He arrived in New Orleans to show his stuff, and his kitten, Paris-Londres, who had accompanied him on his channel race, came, too. He immediately captured the hearts of the city by making an unscheduled flight over the business district. His forty-six-minute flight broke the existing world record for the longest flight over a city.

The last day of the exhibition was touted to be the most memorable. Spectators flowed into City Park. In a show of bravado, Moisant had announced that today, the last day of the year, he would attempt to set the record for the longest sustained flight of 1910, a feat for which he would win the enviable Michelin Cup. To win the cup and the $4,000 prize, he would have to beat the French record of 362.7 miles in 7 hours, 48 minutes, 31 seconds, set by Maurice Tabuteau. Moisant was determined to do it.

He had strapped an additional fuel tank holding 350 gallons of fuel to the monoplane and had scouted out an area, just outside of the city, over which to do his flying. Grandstanders were on the edge of their seats as Moisant's mechanics held tightly on to the tail of the Bleriot while another cranked the propeller and spun the blades. As the motor began to churn, Moisant took off in his plane from City Park and headed west.

The crowd assembled in the Harahan area where Moisant would attempt to break the record watched breathlessly as his plane came into sight. He began to fly around. It looked like the Michelin Cup would surely be his on this day, but as his plane neared the future stockyard site, he hit some turbulence and went into a nosedive. The monoplane was going down. But far worse than the loss of a plane was the loss of life. Not wearing a seat belt, Moisant was thrown from his plane at impact, landing on his head some 36 feet from his beloved aircraft. His neck was broken. He was taken by stretcher to a special train and rushed to the city hospital, where he was pronounced dead. His plane, too, was beyond repair. Moisant was buried in Metairie Cemetery. The New Orleans *Daily Picayune* mourned him as "The King of Aviators."

But that was not all the bad news this day. At approximately the same time that Moisant went down in New Orleans, legendary aviator Arch Hoxsey was killed in an airplane crash in Los Angeles. On January 1, 1911, *The New York Herald* carried the sad news: "John B. Moisant and Arch Hoxsey Drop to Death; Statue Flight Winner Meets Doom at New Orleans, Altitude Champion Crashes to Earth at Los Angeles."

Scientific American reported, "The loss of these two leading aviators, as well as that of Johnstone, will probably tend to retard aviation in America." But the tragedies couldn't stop the momentum. A young aspiring aviator, Clyde Cessna, was waiting in the wings. In February 1911, just a month after Moisant's crash, he used his life savings of $7,500 to purchase the Bleriot-modeled monoplane that was being built for Moisant by the Queen Aeroplane Company in New York.

The Harahan area where Moisant went down was turned into cattle stockyards and then became an airport. To mark the love New Orleans held for Moisant, the airport was named after him and the MSY airport designation stood for Moisant Stock Yards. Even today, though the Moisant airport has been renamed the Louis Armstrong International Airport, baggage tags still sport MSY as the airport's designation.

Matilde Moisant, the second licensed U.S. woman aviator, faced her personal demons, just fifteen months after her brother was killed. Described as a charming, petite woman, devoted to flying, she flew over the same New Orleans field where John Moisant had crashed, awing spectators with her courage and daring. On her last flight, as an act of sisterly love, she flew over the area where her brother was buried and dropped a floral wreath on his grave. Later, she accepted a loving cup from the citizens of the city in honor of her brother and kept it in her living room in loving memory of a city that called John Moisant its own son.

DYNAMITING HELPS SAVE THE CITY

- 1927 -

The citizens of New Orleans were listening for any good news about the flooding upriver. But they didn't get any. Heavy rains and snow in the northern and Midwestern states were dumping an unprecedented amount of water into the Mississippi River. In September 1926 the river's banks began to overflow, and torrential floods hit Nebraska, Kansas, and Iowa. In October the lower part of the river and its tributaries were in danger of flooding, and by the end of the year, every water gauge on the Mississippi, Ohio, and Missouri Rivers had reached record readings.

New Orleanians were extremely anxious, wondering if the river would hold and hoping that if it had to go, it would break somewhere upriver of New Orleans. December brought more bad news as new snowstorms and record-breaking rain found its way into the Mississippi River Valley. By January 1927 the river had reached flood stages at Memphis, Tennessee, and Vicksburg, Mississippi. The flooding was headlined in every newspaper, and on February 2 the Associated Press reported: "Two new breaks in the levees of the St. Francis River added to the distress of flood conditions in eastern Arkansas."

Two days later more than 5,000 people had to flee their homes to seek safety. Little Rock was under water.

Workers in New Orleans had already patched a hole in the levee near the ferry landing on the river, and the washed-out bulkhead at Bayou St. John had been hurriedly repaired. Amid reports of flooded highways and water-covered rail lines, those in power in New Orleans began to rally. It would be up to them to save the city, a thriving business center, which on the best of the driest days lay well below the banks of the river.

By the first day of spring, the levee on the St. Francis River had collapsed, and the Laconia Circle levee in Arkansas had virtually slid into the Mississippi River. Red Cross officials were busy planning refugee camps and procuring army tents for flood victims. All cities along the river posted patrol guards to watch for further leaks in the precarious levee system.

April brought further danger, and on one day, April 15, Good Friday, a religious day of mourning for New Orleans, nearly 18 inches of rain fell in eighteen hours, severely overloading the city's drainage and pumping systems. The city's streetcars were inoperative and every section of the city was flooded. By Saturday morning the Broadmoor area was under 6 feet of water, and Canal Street and the Vieux Carre had 2 feet of water in streets and homes. When the *Inspector,* a molasses tanker, rammed a hole in the levee on April 23, there was widespread panic, and despite the need for food and supplies, boat travel on the river was severely restricted by Louisiana Governor Oramel H. Simpson. More than 22,000 men feverishly worked to bolster the ailing levees between Baton Rouge and New Orleans. Flood victims numbered in the thousands, and disease from the rising water was becoming an urgent problem. Worse, the peak level was not expected for another ten days.

Despite breaks called crevasses along the 1,000 miles of levees on both sides of the river from Cairo, Illinois, to the Gulf of Mexico, by the middle of February the Mississippi in New Orleans had reached flood stage.

But there was a plan starting to surface—one that would save the Crescent City. The problem was that it would also wipe out two areas that sat on the river just below New Orleans. As vehemently as New Orleanians wanted the levee dynamited, the citizens of the affected area refused to accept the destruction of their homes to aid what they considered the rich and powerful political influences in New Orleans. Some even threatened "open warfare."

As the wall of water approached the city in late April, a record flood mark was reached, with a rise of another 4 feet predicted. Something had to give. New Orleanians began to prepare for the worst. They bought boats to carry them and their possessions to safety, and they stockpiled canned goods and medical supplies.

By May the AP reported that most of the Louisiana lowlands were flooded and that watercrafts of all types and sizes were working day and night to rescue the 50,000 men, women, and children of the affected areas. After still another storm dumped 11 inches of rain in two days in the area, fear prevailed everywhere. Even ordinary citizens knew the levees could not hold all the water. Citizens watched the Carrollton river gauge just north of the business district rise higher and higher; New Orleans would be the next stop for the deadly waters. As panic tightened its hold, "Cut the levee below the city" became the city's mantra.

New Orleans was one of the busiest and most influential port cities in the country at this time, and city leaders worried that the destruction brought by floodwaters and their aftermath of cleanup and disease would bring financial ruin. They formed a self-appointed committee and put more and more pressure on the governor to save the city. The final desperate plan was authorized.

A portion of Caernarvon's levee, just 13 miles south of the New Orleans, would be dynamited, allowing water to flood the town and the marshlands of St. Bernard and Plaquemines Parishes, home to many hunters, trappers, and fishermen. From here the water would drain quickly, having easy access to the Gulf of Mexico. Despite a growing argument that the proposed plan would save the wealth and commerce of New Orleans while destroying a less affluent area, the dynamiting would go forward.

The governor, the mayor of New Orleans, the Mississippi River Commission (which had been established by Congress in 1879 to control river flooding), and the army's chief engineer signed off on the proposal. Ten thousand residents of the area were ordered to evacuate their homes. On April 29, 1927, reporters from all over the nation lined the levee for the explosion, but after several blasts only a trickle of water emerged. On May 3 a diver volunteered to set explosive charges under the levee, and thirty-nine tons of dynamite released the raging river and sent 250,000 cubic feet of water per second through the rich, grassy marshlands.

New Orleans escaped major damage, but the lower parishes were devastated. The trappers and farmers of the area were homeless. Fishermen complained of the destruction of the local waterways for several years after the levee was dynamited.

Ironically, as it turned out, because of several major breaks in the levees north of New Orleans, especially a large one that occurred at Cabin Teele on May 2, the deliberate destruction of the Caernarvon levee has been seriously questioned. It was probably unnecessary. Others say it did save the city, estimating the Caernarvon levee crevasse reduced the river's level by as much as 6 feet.

As a result of the devastation of the 1927 flood, the U.S. government passed the 1928 Federal Flood Control Act and took charge of flood control, ensuring the stability of the Mississippi River levee system and the construction of designated spillway areas.

BUILDING THE BOAT THAT WON THE WAR

- 1944 -

THE MOVABLE ASSEMBLY LINES WERE BUSTLING on all floors of the three-story Higgins Industries plant on City Park Avenue. Vitally important to the war effort, the warehouse housed watercraft in every stage of production. Yard after yard, row after row, boats were being assembled at a record pace. Some employees were working on high-speed PT boats; others were hammering out antisubmarine boats, dispatch boats, supply vessels, and specialized patrol craft.

Before World War II Andrew Jackson Higgins had built boats for the oil industry in Louisiana—skiffs that could navigate the shallow bayous and murky swamps of the Louisiana marshes with protected propellers. Higgins had finally broken through the military's bureaucratic red tape and had procured a U.S. Navy contract for his New Orleans boat company. He had to put up some of his own money to build the $12,500 Eureka, as the navy had only awarded him $5,200. He also had to pay shipping charges and a hefty fee to use the navy crane at Norfolk to unload it. But the risk had been worth it; he got the navy order, and the race to build thousands of Landing Craft, Vehicle, Personnel (LCVP) boats was on. By September 1943 the navy boasted 14,000 vessels, of which 13,000 were designed by Higgins and 9,000 had been built in the Higgins plant in New Orleans.

Boats were being built so fast that the streets around the factory had been cordoned off and workers were building ships outside the plant, sometimes in the open air, often under tents. Higgins had also taken over a portion of nearby Holt Cemetery and erected a temporary production space there. They were producing 700 vessels a month (more than all of the rest of the nation's shipyards combined). The boats were so much in demand that Higgins's employees often had to ride on freight trains as ships were being transported, so they could finish the paint job. Higgins was proud of the work produced by his 20,000 employees.

But the main action this summer day was inside the plant.

Louisiana longleaf yellow-pine lumber, personally picked out by timber experts for its huge size and special curvature, was packed high on pallets. Higgins watched as men struggled to pull one of the heavy 40-foot beams into place. The solid block of pine forming the bow, the "headlog," was the strongest part of the boat, making it able to run full speed over obstacles and sandbars. Called the transverse member, it would take the brunt of the landing and give a skiff-type appearance to the boat. The head beam was located just underneath the hinged bow ramp. From there the deep vee-shaped hull flattened out amidships and near the stern reversed to form the semitunnel that protected the propeller and shaft.

Superintendent Graham Haddock, Higgins's draftsman, stood close by. He had worked on many of Higgins's designs and when the high-spirited entrepreneur had said, "I had a dream last night, and I want you to put it on paper," Haddock had risen to the task.

As Higgins strode to the next station, he found a LCVP almost finished. The strong durable wood from Louisiana forests had been joined with oak, mahogany, and steel to make up the boxy, shallow boat. It was almost ready for the application of thick coats of gray military paint. The Higgins factory was the first to have an integrated workforce where blacks and whites, men and women, worked side by side. To keep his plant going and to build as many boats as possible, he paid top wages to all, including retired persons and those with physical disabilities.

Higgins marched past the huge banner hung high above the work area where everyone could read: THE MAN WHO RELAXES IS HELPING THE AXIS. He neared a large group of men and women who stood looking at an enormous gray boat. Congratulating themselves on a job well done, they stood back to admire the boat's 36-foot length and 30-foot width. It weighed 9 tons. The shallow-draft skiff could navigate in only 18 inches of water and run over debris or sea vegetation without clogging its propeller. It could run right up to shore and back itself away without hurting the hull. The LCVP was fashioned after the Higgins Eureka boat, which could jump floating logs as well as ride up the stone steps of the Lake Pontchartrain seawall and make sharp turns at top speed.

Workers felt relief that this particular "Higgins boat," as it would be called by the troops, was now completed and set for shipment. The boat was ready to run up to the beaches of Europe and could carry fully armed troops, light tanks, field artillery, and other equipment and supplies. It would reach less fortified, shallow beaches, eliminating the need to sweep harbors for mines or take over enemy ports. Made entirely out of wood except for its steel landing ramp, the LCVP could carry an entire platoon of thirty-six men or a Jeep and supplies right up to the beach, unload in seconds, and pull out just as quickly, ready to pick up another contingent of troops and equipment.

It would make history as it stormed over the beaches of Normandy on June 6, 1944.

Higgins was in Chicago on D-Day, but he knew his employers would be anxious over the role their ships would play in the massive amphibious landings. He wired his employees and ordered his message to be broadcast over the factory's loudspeaker. He told his workers: "Now the work of our hands, our hearts, and our heads is being put to the test."

Throughout the war the LCVPs would land at Normandy, Guadalcanal, Tarawa, Iwo Jima, Okinawa, Leyte, Guam, and hundreds of other battlefields in the European and Pacific Theaters.

Higgins boats were lauded as vital to the winning of the war. Historian Colonel Joseph H. Alexander, USMC, said, "The Higgins boats broke the gridlock on the ship-to-shore movement. It is impossible to overstate the tactical advantage his craft gave U.S. amphibious commanders in World War II."

Hitler, foiled on all fronts by Higgins boats, called Higgins the "new Noah."

Although he was often cantankerous and headstrong, Higgins proved that his ships, designed and built in a small southern shipyard, could compete with the nation's best.

On November 23, 1944, months after the D-Day invasion, Higgins workers sitting around radios after their Thanksgiving meal were surprised to hear General Dwight D. Eisenhower, supreme commander of the Allied forces, express his appreciation of their tireless efforts in his address to the nation: "Let us thank God for Higgins Industries, management, and labor, which has given us the landing boats with which to conduct our campaign." Eisenhower said of Andrew Jackson Higgins, "He is the man who won the war for us."

Higgins was awarded the Army–Navy "E" Award, the highest award given to a businessperson.

During the war Higgins was also a subcontractor on the top-secret Manhattan Project. Called to Washington, D.C., by President Franklin D. Roosevelt, he was told that for seven months no one had been able to successfully manufacture the needed parts for the atomic bomb. The president challenged Higgins. The Michoud facility in New Orleans was selected for its high security, and every employee was required to take an oath of secrecy. All bomb parts that were made of carbon were manufactured in New Orleans.

After the war Higgins tried to keep his employees on the payroll for as long as he could. He eventually began manufacturing helicopters and leisure vehicles. A reproduction of the D-Day landing craft is on display at the D-Day Museum in New Orleans. It was built entirely by volunteers, World War II veterans, former Higgins employees, and other enthusiasts who rescued a sunken Higgins boat from Irish Bayou south of New Orleans to use as a model.

AT THE END OF A STREETCAR LINE

- 1946 -

The 1940s were vibrant years for New Orleans. The French Market teemed with vendors offering all sorts of unique commodities from okra by the pound to endive roots, known as chicory. The Café du Monde served hot steaming coffee and sugary powdered beignets all hours of the day and night. Lavish hotels catered to wealthy tourists. Pontchartrain Beach, an amusement park north of the city, was a popular place for couples trying to forget the vicissitudes of war. The city was working on updating its transportation system, replacing the slow steam-powered streetcars with more efficient buses, but that wouldn't happen until the end of the decade, thank goodness.

Thomas Lanier Williams had lived on Toulouse Street for a few months in the spring of 1938 and, more importantly, he had changed his name here. So when the now-famous Tennessee Williams arrived in town in 1946, it was like coming home. For his stay in the City that Care Forgot, Williams rented a small apartment in the French Quarter at 632 St. Peter Street. The room had a latticed balcony that overlooked the vibrant, bustling city, and from here he could watch the comings and goings of colorful and eccentric characters. He could hear the old wood-and-steel "arch roof" streetcars rattling on rails set in cobblestone along Bourbon and Royal Streets. As a writer, he put his observations to paper, describing the noise as "that rattle-trap of a streetcar that bangs up one old street and down another."

In his third-floor apartment, Williams settled into a routine. He would have his morning coffee, then sit at the table under a skylight and write for most of the day. He was writing a play based on a card game metaphor in which one of the main characters, Blanche, hid her past indiscretions behind a poker face of southern gentility. He was considering three titles: *Poker Night, The Moth,* and *Blanche's Chair on the Moon.* While he wrote, Williams liked to listen to music, but the noisy streetcar continued to bang along the street at 9 miles per hour, often distracting him from his work.

Sometimes for lunch he would venture down to Galatoire's Restaurant on Royal Street, known for its starched white tablecloths and tuxedoed waiters. He would glide over to his favorite corner table by the window and leisurely enjoy the authentic French Creole cuisine. Galatoire's was an energetic dining place where locals chattered and called to each other from across the room.

In late afternoon Williams would take a break from his writing, which he referred to as "the rigors of creation." He frequently wandered the Vieux Carre to experience the ebullient street life. Sometimes he would stroll around the corner to Victor's restaurant to hear "If I Didn't Care" by the Ink Spots on the jukebox while sipping a brandy Alexander. Most days he would go the New Orleans Athletic Club on Rampart Street and get some exercise swimming in the indoor pool. One afternoon he went with his friend Pancho down to the Pennyland Arcade at 209 Bourbon Street. Amidst the clanking pinball machines, the duo recorded their amateur singing and reciting in a Voice-O-Graph booth.

Every day Williams was back banging on his typewriter, trying to wrap up the new play. He settled on *Poker Night* as the title. But still something was missing. Williams's attention often turned to the ever-intrusive streetcars rambling up and down the French Quarter. He noticed not only the noise made by the durable Perley A. Thomas Car Works trolleys and their mesmerizing side-to-side sway, but also their intriguing names. Streetcars in New Orleans were named not by numbers or colors as other systems in the country, but by their destination.

Williams thought a lot about the streetcars passing so close to his apartment. Having fought the intrusion for too long, he decided to embrace the clanging bells and grumbling motors and drew inspiration from their meanderings. He said, "Their indiscouragable progress up and down Royal Street struck me as having some symbolic bearing of a broad nature on the life in the Vieux Carre."

Looking up to the placard on the front of the streetcar that ran through the seedier side of the French Quarter, Williams read "Desire." When the Desire line intersected with the Cemeteries line on Canal Street, Williams discovered a perfect metaphor for the contradictions of life.

Williams changed the name of his new play from *Poker Night* to *A Streetcar Named Desire,* and Blanche's famous lines, "They told me to take a streetcar named Desire, and then transfer to one called Cemeteries and ride six blocks and get off at—Elysian Fields!" became a part of literary history.

As Williams gave himself up to the sights and sounds of New Orleans, the play took shape. Characters Blanche and Mitch would venture to Pontchartrain Beach on their date in act 2, and Stella would take sister Blanche to Galatoire's for supper. Mitch would work out with weights at the New Orleans Athletic Club, and Stella and Stanley would live in a run-down apartment on Elysian Fields in

Faubourg Marigny, an area just outside the French Quarter. When Tennessee Williams remarked to Pancho that many of the people he often invited over to the small apartment weren't even good friends, Pancho reportedly answered, "Some of my best friends are strangers," foreshadowing the play's most famous line, "I've always depended on the kindness of strangers."

A Streetcar Named Desire premiered to rave reviews in New York City on December 3, 1947, and heralded the creative genius of Tennessee Williams.

The last Desire streetcar ran on May 30, 1948. It was replaced by a bus line also called Desire. Other New Orleans places can be found throughout Williams's works. The picturesque courtyard of the Hotel Maison de Ville is said to have provided the inspiration for the *Night of the Iguana* set, and the interior overgrown garden of a friend was used in *Suddenly Last Summer.*

Williams called New Orleans his favorite city in the world and explained: "In New Orleans I found the kind of freedom I had always needed. And the shock of it against the Puritanism of my nature has always given me a subject, a theme, which I've probably never ceased exploiting."

Williams's stays in New Orleans were productive times because, he said, "In New York eccentrics are ignored; in L.A. they're arrested, but in New Orleans [they're] allowed to develop their eccentricities into art."

New Orleans was for Williams as Paris was for Hemingway and Fitzgerald. He lovingly reflected, "If I can be said to have a home, it is in New Orleans."

ANOTHER DAY AT SCHOOL

- 1960 -

On this day of "firsts," six-year-old Ruby was wearing a white starched dress, new white shoes, and a special white ribbon in her hair. Today she would be attending William Frantz Public School on Alvar Street in the Florida neighborhood of New Orleans. Ruby Nell Bridges knew her new school would be different; she had taken a special test and had overheard her mother and father praying for her in church. Ruby was excited, but what a fuss was being made!

Just after breakfast, four white men in neatly pressed suits with yellow deputy U.S. marshal armbands showed up at her house in big black cars to take her and her mother to school. Ruby thought that was very odd, but what she didn't know was that she would be making history on her first day as a first grader. She would be the first black child to attend the all-white William Frantz School, the first school to be integrated in New Orleans.

When they arrived at the school, Ruby peered intently out of the car window. The tall brick school building loomed large, and, she thought, looked much nicer than her kindergarten school over on Law Street. Then Ruby saw the barricades and policemen lining the street. She hadn't been afraid before, but now she wasn't sure if she liked this new school. The crowds seemed to be closing in on her. People were shouting and waving posters in her face. The marshals rushed her and her mother out of the car, up the front steps, and into the school as fast as they could. Ruby thought her new school must be an important place.

That first day she and her mother spent their time in the principal's office. Ruby saw many white parents screaming and arguing as they dragged their children out of classrooms up and down the hall. Ruby and her mother waited and then waited some more. In fact that was all they did that day. They didn't talk to anyone, and they didn't go to Ruby's classroom. They just watched the big clock on the wall, and when it said 3:00 P.M., Ruby and her mother stood up and the same marshals escorted them out of the school and down the steps to the waiting cars.

The crowd outside was now bigger than it had been that morning. Teenage boys were waving Confederate flags, and women held up posters of Governor Jimmy Davis, who vowed to close down the public schools in Louisiana rather than integrate them. Some kids were singing songs with newly made-up racist verses, but Ruby was especially frightened by the people displaying a black doll lying in a makeshift coffin. It took a long time to get to the waiting cars.

The second day of school was tough. The marshals again took Ruby and her mother to school. The crowds had assembled once again shouting terrible things at the young girl. One woman threatened to poison Ruby. But there was a bright spot. Today, Ruby met her first grade teacher, Mrs. Henry, a young white woman with kind eyes. When she took Ruby up to her classroom, Ruby was confused. There were rows of desks, but they were all empty. There were no other children in the school; angry parents had kept them home.

Mrs. Barbara Henry and Ruby were alone in the classroom, and they would remain that way the entire school year. A few other white children did return to the school after a while, but they were sent to other rooms and taught by other teachers. Ruby liked Mrs. Henry instantly and loved learning, although she found it hard to understand why she wasn't allowed to go to the cafeteria for lunch or take recess outside, and she thought having federal marshals escort her to the bathroom was weird.

On the third day of school, her mother had to take care of her brothers and sister. She said, "Ruby, I can't go to school with you today, but don't be afraid. The marshals will take care of you. Be good now, and don't cry."

The little girl had already begun to cry.

When she opened her front door a few minutes later, Ruby looked up at the marshals and resolved to do what her mother had said. She later explained, "I was the Ruby who had to do it—go into that school and stay there, no matter what those people said."

Ruby had hoped it would be different today. But it wasn't. It was worse. There were more people than she had ever seen before, and they were yelling and throwing things at her. She was very fearful and didn't understand what was happening. The hateful throngs showed up day after day. One morning when she was nearly surrounded by the teeming crowd, Ruby realized something was wrong. She had forgotten to say her prayers before heading off to school. Her mother had always told her that prayers worked miracles. She had said, "Ruby, if I'm not with you and you're afraid, then always say your prayers."

So Ruby stopped short. She faced the unruly crowd, looked straight at the menacing protestors . . . and said her prayers.

Please, God, try to forgive those people
Because even if they say those bad things,
They don't know what they're doing.
So You could forgive them,
Just like You did those folks a long time ago
When they said terrible things about You.

The crowd thought Ruby was addressing them. They started shouting even louder. As Ruby finished her prayers, the marshals spirited her away quickly into the school building. She ran upstairs to her second-floor classroom where Mrs. Henry waited to give her a big hug to start the day. She asked Ruby why she had stopped to talk to the people out front. Ruby explained to Mrs. Henry that she hadn't been talking to the crowd; she had been talking to God.

Ruby learned that the trouble in New Orleans was not just at her school. Across the city angry mobs roamed the streets throwing bricks, rocks, even gasoline-filled bottles at cars and businesses. The Klu Klux Klan burned crosses in black neighborhoods as threats and warnings. Vandals destroyed black businesses. Ruby's family was punished for its role in desegregation. The locally owned white grocery store refused to wait on her mother, and her father lost his job.

Despite the protests, the schools in New Orleans were never closed down completely. John Steinbeck wrote about Ruby's experience at the William Frantz School in *Travels with Charley.* The artist Norman Rockwell was moved by Steinbeck's description of Ruby's ordeal and drew *The Problem We All Live With,* a painting of the little school girl flanked by the marshals; tomatoes are being thrown at her white dress, white shoes, and special hair ribbon. Ruby returned to the same school in the fall, but this time there were no demonstrations and no federal escorts.

BURYING THE MUSICIAN

- 2004 -

Lloyd James Washington, last member of the legendary Ink Spots, a popular group in the 1950s and 1960s, died on June 22, 2004, at the age of eighty-three. Because there was no money to pay for his burial, his remains were cremated and put in a small box. And where in New Orleans would the ashes of a renowned musician end up? At a local bar, of course!

Well, not just any bar and not without fanfare. His widow, with the wooden jewelry box nestled in her arms, rode in a pink limousine to the Ernie K-Doe Mother-in-Law Lounge, a bright-blue two-story clapboard house on North Claiborne Avenue operated by Antoinette K-Doe. She placed the box of Washington's ashes in front of the life-like, pink-suited mannequin of the late Ernie K-Doe, a prominent musician himself, who ruled over the scene from his tinseled throne. The makeshift shrine, under a ceiling of paper stars, was bedecked with statues of angels and lit by candles. It seemed a fitting spot for the time being for Washington, a beloved figure in the New Orleans music world. During the last years of his life, he had played gigs at the nearby Palm Court Jazz Cafe and at the House of Blues over in the French Quarter. An Ink Spots album cover was also set in place as a tribute to the musician. But everyone agreed that a more permanent spot must be found soon for the musician's ashes.

Anna Ross Twichell was a licensed cemetery tour guide in the very touristy city of New Orleans, where even tombs are sights to see. One day, as she escorted a group of neck-stretching voyeurs through the narrow streets in the "city of the dead," she had a brainstorm. She knew that in another part of town, the Barbarin family of celebrated musicians owned a huge burial vault that was mostly unused and in need of restoration. She set a plan to help with the repairs if the family was willing to allow musicians without resources to be laid to rest in a section of their tomb.

In New Orleans many of the old aboveground tombs fell into disuse because of centuries of neglect. More than 80 percent of the graves have no known relatives of those interred to help maintain the gravesites. Other sites, like the mausoleum of the Barbarin family, descendents of jazz pioneer and Onward Brass Band leader Isidore Barbarin, are city landmarks, though still in need of repair. Theirs is a centuries-old, eighteen-vault, 14-foot-7-inch-high structure located along the St. Louis Street side of St. Louis Cemetery No. 1. One of the unique features of the mausoleums in New Orleans is that after interment of a year and a day, a body can be taken out of its casket, reburied in a bag, and settled into the caveau, a shallow holding area beneath the tomb, in order to create space for more caskets above. There is plenty of room for the sacred ashes of many cremated bodies.

On July 16, 2004, when Al "Carnival Time" Johnson went to the Ernie K-Doe Mother-in-Law Lounge for a fish fry, he met up with Twichell and the Barbarins. Twichell had convinced the Barbarins to donate a portion of their family vault as a final resting place for the city's indigent musicians. Beneath the crowded display of Ernie K-Doe photographs and memorabilia at the Mother-in-Law Lounge and under the watchful eyes of Washington's ashes, Johnson served as witness to the signing of documents that would establish the Barbarin vault as the New Orleans Musicians Tomb. Now and in the future, any New Orleans musician who wished to could rest among his peers. When all the papers had been signed in the back room of her Ernie K-Doe Lounge, proprietor Antoinette K-Doe asked, "So that means Lloyd can go in the tomb?"

At the affirmative nod from the attorney present, she sighed, "Good. 'Cause I'm tired of him sleeping here."

The hot humid Saturday, October 23, 2004, was a momentuous day. Lloyd Washington's ashes had rested long enough at the Ernie K-Doe Mother-in-Law Lounge. Friends placed his box of ashes in a casket and loaded it in the back of a red pickup truck. Flowers, palms, and Mardi Gras beads adorned the casket tied with netting to the back of the truck. Mourners were decked out in their finest clothes for the day's activities and had gathered at St. Augustine's Church, an imposing stone edifice on Governor Nicholls Street in the historic Treme neighborhood to await his arrival. Melodic strains rang out in moving vocal tributes performed by local singers.

After the solemn service the festive celebrants moved forward, forming a "second line" funeral procession to Louis Cemetery No. 1 on Basin Street. It was time to celebrate. There was even a couple of "baby dolls" in attendance—women dressed as babies, a New Orleans tradition, recalling the costumes worn by "uptown" ladies of the evening who marched in Mardi Gras parades back in the 1920s. Clapping hands and dancing feet escorted the ashes of famed musician Lloyd Washington in his final parade through the city. By 1:00 P.M. gravesite mourners, gathered in front of the Barbarin vault for the dedication ceremony, had quieted. Friends and well-wishers listened to guest speakers and city dignitaries laud Washington, who would be the first musician to be buried in the New Orleans Musicians Tomb. His silver and black urn, protected by two porcelain angels, was placed in the crypt, which already held the remains of drummer Lucien and trumpeter Charles, musician ancestors of the Barbarins. His widow, Hazel, raised her index finger skyward, then let it fall, finally "signifying the release of her late husband's spirit."

Money collected at a "Dyin' To Get In" fund-raiser at the New Orleans Mid-City Lanes Rock 'n' Bowl nightclub helped to restore the old dilapidated cemetery mausoleum now called the Musicians Tomb. In true New Orleans style, donors threw dollar bills into the symbolic velvet coffin that mock pallbearers paraded around the dance floor. Funds would also go toward erecting a memorial plaque listing the names of the New Orleans musicians entombed in the vault.

AND THE WATER RUSHED THROUGH THE CITY

- 2005 -

Nervous citizens were glued to their televisions for days tracking mighty Katrina. She had begun as a tropical depression on August 23, 2005. Strengthening into a hurricane, she headed to the southern coast of Florida, but crossing over land did not diminish Katrina's wrath, and as she entered the warm waters of the Gulf of Mexico, she intensified.

Familiar with hurricanes, people in cities and towns along the Louisiana coast began to board up their homes and businesses. They packed personal necessities, booked hotel rooms and notified relatives that evacuation might ensue.

By August 28, Katrina was at her peak, a category 5 hurricane barreling towards the Gulf Coast. She was not only an extremely strong hurricane; she was a life-threatening storm expected to affect a broad area.

Dire reports warned that if New Orleans sustained a direct blow from Katrina, there would be "complete roof failure on many residences and industrial buildings . . . some complete building failures . . . severe and extensive window and door damage . . . major damage to lower floors of all structures."

Forecasters predicted rising water would turn the city into a huge toxic lake filled with chemicals and human waste as levees gave way, septic systems failed, and sewer lines caved in.

Fear permeated the city built below sea level.

As Katrina moved northward toward New Orleans with winds of over 140 miles per hour, citizens evacuated to higher ground. Baton Rouge, Houston, Austin, Montgomery, and other surrounding towns opened shelters and took in evacuees. Conditions deteriorated rapidly, and the Crescent City braced herself for one of the most powerful storms of the century.

At the eleventh hour, when it seemed New Orleans would not be spared, Mayor Ray Nagin announced a mandatory evacuation of the city's 500,000 residents. Most headed out of the city. But for more than 100,000 citizens without money, means of transportation, or physical and mental ability, it was already too late. Families, friends, and strangers hunkered down in homes, office buildings, hospitals, and other structures thought to be the most protective. They hoped Katrina would be merciful.

Katrina plowed into the Louisiana coast at daybreak on Monday, August 29, 2005, bringing high winds and blinding rain. Trees snapped in two. Hundred-year-old oaks were pulled up by their roots. Windows blew out of homes and offices. Wind sheered off pieces of buildings and hurled lost shingles and roof tiles through the air. Dead pigeons littered the roadways. Streetlights lay shattered. Natural gas lines began to leak and power poles stood at 45-degree angles.

But despite the wreckage, New Orleans had stared the enemy in the face and won. Due to a slight eastern jog and decrease in wind speed, New Orleans had been spared. Stories of inevitable death and destruction seemed just that, stories.

As the rain abated, those holed up in the city ventured out to evaluate the destruction, and evacuees began their trek home.

Then the unthinkable happened.

As Katrina passed north of New Orleans, a 20-foot surge in Lake Pontchartrain headed south toward the city. Floodwaters began to erode earthen embankments, causing the concrete walls of the hurricane protection levees to bulge outwards. Cracks appeared in the concrete sections, which tilted, shifted, and eventually gave way. The London Avenue Canal failed, flooding Gentilly and surrounding neighborhoods. At the same time surge waters flooded into the 17th Street Canal, and this system, too, failed, pouring water into West End, the city's seafood haven on the banks of Lake Pontchartrain. For miles, homes were visible only as roofs floating in a sea of murky water. Interstate 10 exit ramps resembled boat ramps leading down not to streets but to swirling waters.

By 7:45 A.M., less than three hours after Katrina made landfall, the levees of the imposing Industrial Canal were also breached. An explosive wall of water inundated more neighborhoods of New Orleans East, Lakeview, Chalmette, Meraux, Violet, the Lower Ninth Ward, and St. Bernard.

Exploding transformers lit up the early morning skies as electric lines went dead. Police and fire rescue team efforts were severely limited. Broken water mains and contamination meant that drinking water was unavailable throughout the city. Trash and garbage bobbed in the water. Murky water lapped at roof shingles. Looting began; lawlessness took hold of the Big Easy.

Thousands of people found themselves stranded without food and water. When water reached rooftops, many who had fled to second stories or attics found themselves trapped. Frantic cell phone callers begged for help. Hundreds clawed and hacked their way out and perched on rooftops desperately signaling to hovering helicopters.

People waded through waist-high water in search of aid. Some carried babies or elderly family members in their arms. Others floated the infirm and aged on rafts or makeshift pallets. Thousands of people had made it to the Superdome to weather the storm, and now they were joined by still more victims in search of help and a dry place to stay. The hot, humid days of August made the stifling air inside the Superdome almost unbearable. Thousands of victims were also huddled in the huge convention center at the foot of Canal Street for days without water or security. Stories of death, crime, and hopelessness were reported.

The images of the city during this catastrophe ran the gamut from the black body bags lining the streets, the putrid Superdome, and anarchy and chaos, to outstretched helping hands, dedicated rescue workers, shared food and water, and the relieved faces of reunited family members.

The floods could not be stopped, and by August 31 nearly 80 percent of New Orleans was under 6 to 9 feet of standing, fetid water.

In the aftermath of Katrina, the city coped with widespread devastation and human need. Citizens with few possessions and nowhere to go were transported out of the city. The collection and identification of the dead began. Water was pumped out of inundated neighborhoods. Levee repairs were begun. Hundreds of volunteers rushed to the city to search for the missing. Supplies for victims and first responders were donated. Thousands of animals were rescued. Reporters roamed the devastated city bringing its sad story to the outside world.

But Mother Nature was not finished with New Orleans yet. A new storm had entered the gulf.

As Hurricane Rita approached the Louisiana–Texas border, search and rescue was suspended in the nearly empty city. Water was again pouring through levee breaches. Land pumped dry was again flooded. Evacuees who had fled to the areas now in Rita's path had to evacuate again. New Orleans was once again under a state of emergency.

When the weather finally cleared, New Orleans was a devastated ghost town. Neighborhoods flooded by contaminated water stood empty. Businesses were closed. Trade and tourism were at a standstill. The Superdome sat bruised and battered. The wrought-iron balconies of the French Quarter lay twisted and discarded. The storm forced the shutdown of over a million barrels of refining capacity, and gasoline prices spiked throughout the nation. A million people were left homeless, and it was predicted that many would never return to their lives in the City that Care Forgot. More than 1,000 people, mostly elderly, died in the New Orleans Katrina disaster.

For more than 250 years, settlers and traders, businessmen and women, families, and renegades had been lured to the mysterious, marshy city at the mouth of the Mississippi River. City officials had assured their citizens that pumps, canals, and a protective levee system would keep floodwater from their doorsteps. They kept that promise until August 29, 2005.

REFERENCES

Playing a Trick on the English—1699

"Jean Baptiste Le Moyne, Sieur de Bienville, 1680–1767." *Encyclopedia Louisiana.* www.enlou.com/people/bienville-bio.htm (accessed January 29, 2005).

Kukla, Jon. "History: 1699." *Louisiana Lifestyle Magazine Online,* www.louisiana101.com/rr_1699_lalife.html (accessed October 26, 2004).

Lighting a Candle and Saying a Prayer—1788

"Early History, Chapter II: The Year of Calamity." The Saint Louis Cathedral, www.stlouiscathedral.org/HistoryE2.htm (accessed November 8, 2005).

"Louisiana Timeline." *Encyclopedia Louisiana,* www.enlou.com/time/year1788.htm (accessed November 8, 2005).

Reeves, Sally. "French Quarter Fire and Flood." New Orleans French Quarter, www.frenchquarter.com/history/elements.php (accessed November 8, 2005).

Singing into History—1796

Belsom, Jack. "Historical Milestones of Opera in New Orleans." New Orleans Opera Association, www.neworleansopera.org (accessed August 6, 2005).

Kane, Harnett T. *Queen New Orleans, City by the River.* New York: William Morrow & Company, 1949.

Parrillo, Vincent N. *Diversity in America,* 2nd ed. California: Pine Forge Press, 1996.

Strickland, Eliza. "Making History Sing." *Gambit Weekly,* www.bestofneworleans.com/dispatch/2003-09-30/ae_feat.html (accessed August 5, 2005).

Vella, Christina. *Intimate Enemies.* Baton Rouge: Louisiana State University Press, 1997.

The Stars and Stripes Wave over the City—1803

Ambrose, Stephen E. and Douglas Brinkley. "Current Events." *Gambit Weekly,* 64.233.161.104/search?q=cache:PRdEMBj2ZTgJ:www.bestofneworleans.com/dispatch/2001-08-21/cover_story.html+Louisiana+Purchase+2001&hl=en (accessed November 17, 2005).

Hitchcock, Ripley. "Chapter VIII: Transfer to the United States." In *The Louisiana Purchase and the Exploration, Early History and Building of the West.* Boston: Ginn & Company Publishers, The Athenaeum Press, 1903. Also available at www.usgennet.org/usa/topic/preservation/history/louis/chpt8.htm (accessed November 17, 2005).

Lewis, Ralph. "The Louisiana Purchase, Part IV—Possessing the New Land." www.nps.gov/jeff/LewisClark2/TheBicentennial/Symposium2002/Papers/Lewis_Ralph.htm (accessed November 17, 2005).

"The Louisiana Purchase, 1803." *The Louisiana Purchase, A Heritage Explored, Historical Perspectives, 1682–1815,* www.lib.lsu

.edu/special/purchase/history.html (accessed November 17, 2005).

The Scales of Justice Are Slightly Tilted—1830

"All Hail the Queen." www.parascope.com/en/articles/voodooQueen 01.htm (accessed June 11, 2006).

Arbury, David. "Marie Laveau Biography." ame2.asu.edu/sites/ voodoodreams/marie_laveau.asp (accessed October 26, 2004).

Tallant, Robert. *Voodoo in New Orleans.* New York: The Macmillan Company, 1946.

A New Orleans Fishing Tale—1840

Landry, Stuart Omer. *Dueling in Old New Orleans.* New Orleans: Harmanson, 1950.

Schwab, Lucille-Nichols. C. Howard Collection, Box 6, Article 114. www2.selu.edu/Academics/Depts/RegionalStudies/archival coll/S/schwab-nichols-scrapbooks.html (accessed August 5, 2005).

Stall, Buddy. "A Dueling Loophole: Harpoons at 20 Paces." *Clarion Herald,* September 16, 1999.

A Small Boy Looks into His Future—1845

"Charles Henry Stanley vs. Eugene Rousseau Match." members.aol .com/graemecree/chesschamps/us/1845.htm (accessed June 2, 2005).

McCrary, Robert John. "The Forgotten Forties." www.chess museum.org/history0399.html (accessed June 2, 2005).

"Paul Morphy: The Life and Chess of Paul Morphy." www.angel fire.com/games/SBChess/Morphy/Paul_Morphy.html (accessed June 2, 2005).

Bronze John, an Unwelcome Visitor—1853

"Arrival of the Sierra Nevada! Letter from New York and New Orleans, Ravages of the Yellow Fever, Foreign and Domestic News." *Daily Alta California.* The Maritime Heritage Project: Ships, Captains, Passengers into San Francisco, www.maritime heritage.org/PassLists/sn091553.htm (accessed June 15, 2005).

"Bronze John: Yellow fever's deadly visits to New Orleans." New Orleans in affiliation with the *Times-Picayune.* www.nola.com/haunted/rue/morgue_yellow.html (accessed October 30, 2004).

"The History of Our Lady of Guadalupe Chapel." International Shrine of St. Jude Our Lady of Guadalupe Chapel, New Orleans, Louisiana, www.saintjudeshrine.com/history.htm (accessed June 15, 2005).

Exposing More than the Truth—1853

Kane, Harnett T. *Queen New Orleans, City by the River.* New York: William Morrow & Company, 1949.

Murray, Henry A. *Lands of the Slave and the Free.* Fullbooks. www.fullbooks.com/Lands-of-the-Slave-and-the-Free4.html (accessed September 9, 2005).

Seymour, Bruce. Chronological Documentation for 1853. http://www.zpub.com/sf/history/lola/Bc1853.doc (accessed September 10, 2005).

"The Spider Dance of Lola Montez." www.uq.edu.au/~entjohns/spider.html, and click "proceed" (accessed September 9, 2005).

Riding for the Glory—1854

"Fairgrounds Race Course." www.fairgroundsracecourse.com/about/history.html (accessed July 24, 2005).

"The Great State Post Stake." *New York Daily Times,* Apr. 11, 1854. Reprinted from the New Orleans *Daily Picayune,* April 2, 1854.

Mershon, J. H. "Notation on a file of the Second Regiment Kansas Volunteers—Cavalry, Company L." From files of Farron L. Kempton, biographer.

"Rice's Derby Choice Journal 2005—26th Edition." www.innisfree.org/2005.html (accessed August 27, 2005).

Light as Air—1855

"Louis Moreau Gottschalk (1829–1869) Piano Music—6." www.hypherion-records.co.uk/notes/67349-N.asp (accessed July 21, 2005).

New Orleans Daily Delta. Ad for balloon rides. January 1, 1855, p. 3, col. 1. www.uttyl.edu/vbetts/new_orleans_daily_delta_1855.htm (accessed July 22, 2005).

Virgets, Ronnie. "Virgets: King Louis." *Gambit Weekly.* www.bestofneworleans.com/dispatch/2001-12-18/views-virgets.html (accessed July 21, 2005).

Whistling Dixie—1861

"Dixie (I Wish I Was in Dixie Land)" and "A short history of Daniel Decatur Emmett and 'Dixie.'" www.seriesam.com/barks/deta_text_s_dixie.html (accessed September 11, 2005).

Kane, G. A. "Dan Emmett Its Author and New York the Place of Its Production." Richmond *Dispatch,* March 19, 1893.

Schrechengost, Gary. "Wheat's Tigers: Confederate Zouaves at First Manassas." *America's Civil War Magazine,* www.historynet.com/acw/blzouaves-tigers/ (accessed September 11, 2005).

Ward, A. W., A .R. Waller, W. P. Trent, J. Erskine, S. P. Sherman, and C. Van Doren (eds.). "Poets of the Civil War II, Dixie: The Bonnie Blue Flag." *The Cambridge History of English and American Literature: An Encyclopedia in Eighteen Volumes,* Volume XVI. New York: G. P. Putnam's Sons; Cambridge, England: University Press, 1907–1921.

Confederate Spy Slips Away Again—1863

Sasser, Bill. "Lady in Gray." *Gambit Weekly.* Cover Story, September 14, 2004. www.bestofneworleans.com/dispatch/2004-09-14/cover_story.html (accessed November 6, 2004).

Velazquez, Loreta Janeta. *The Woman in Battle.* Richmond, Va.: Dustin, Gilman & Co., 1876.

Cold Storage Enhances Fine Dining—1869

"June 10—Today in Science History." www.todayinsci.com (accessed August 20, 2005).

New Orleans Daily Delta. Letter to the Editor from Sally Ann Doesticks. January 22, 1855, p. 3, col. 3. www.uttyl.edu/vbetts/new_orleans_daily_delta_1855.htm (accessed July 21, 2005).

"Refrigeration." *The Handbook of Texas Online,* www.tsha.utexas.edu/handbook/online/articles/RR/dqr1_print.html (accessed July 21, 2005).

"She Takes the Horns"—1870

"Man piloted the Robert E. Lee to fame." *Messenger-Inquirer,* www.messengerinquirer.com/specialarchives/connections/7618356.htm

"The Natchez and the Robert E. Lee." http://www.oldandsold.com/article01/article852.shtml (accessed October 18, 2004).

Way, Frederick Jr. *She Takes the Horns: Steamboat Racing on the Western Waves.* Cincinnati: The Picture Marine Library Publishing Company, Young & Klein, 1953.

Degas Misses His Train—1872

Benfey, Christopher. "Chris Benfey Writes about Painter Edgar Degas' Life in the Nineteenth-Century 'Big Easy.'" *The College Street Journal,* www.mtholyoke.edu/offices/comm/csj/980123/benfey.html (accessed November 20, 2004).

Feigenbaum, Gail. "Degas in New Orleans—New Orleans Museum of Art." *USA Today (Society for the Advancement of Education),* July 1999.

Loveitt, Bruce. "Review of Christopher E. G. Benfey's *Degas in New Orleans.*" www.amazon.com/gp/product/customer-reviews/0520218183/ref=cm_cr_dp_pt/102-1167356-1169719?%5Fencoding=UTF8&n=283155&s=books (accessed November 20, 2004).

Wibking, Angela. "New Orleans' Degas exhibit smartly combines art and tourism." *Weekly Wire, Nashville Scene,* www.weeklywire.com/ww/07-26-99/nash_8-art.html (accessed November 19, 2004).

The Spirit of the Sultan's Palace—1873

Danahy, Barbara. "Murder at the Sultan's Palace." www.nola.com/haunted/harem/hauntings/murder.html (accessed August 24, 2005).

"Haunted New Orleans." New Orleans Paranormal & Occult Research Society Ghostly Gallery. www.neworleansghosts.com/haunted_new_orleans.htm (accessed August 24, 2005).

Meadows-Galloway, Nancy A. "New Orleans Ghost Tour: A Hauntingly Good Time!" www.finetuning.com/articles/p3-925-new-orleans-ghost-tour-a-hauntingly-good-time.html (accessed August 4, 2005).

Ringing in Prosperity—1884

Charters, Samuel Barclay, IV. *Jazz: New Orleans 1885–1963.* New York: Da Capo Press, 1983.

Paige, John C. "The Liberty Bell of Independence National Historic Park: A Special History Study," National Park Service. "1885 World's Industrial and Cotton Centennial Exposition." www.libertybellmuseum.com/WorldsFair/1885.htm (accessed September 24, 2005).

"The World's Fair and Exposition Information and Reference Guide." www.earthstation9.com/index.html?worlds_2.htm (accessed September 24, 2005).

Black Indians Parade through Town—1885

"Mardi Gras Indians." Mardi Gras Louisiana State Museum/ Canadian Heritage Information Network. www.virtualmuseum.ca/Exhibitions/Festiva1/en/lsm/page3.html (accessed September 24, 2005).

"Mardi Gras Quotes." Mardi Gras Unmasked. www.mardigrasunmasked.com/mardigras/carnival_quotes.htm (accessed October 6, 2005).

Medley, Keith Weldon. "From Sire to Son—From Chief to Chief." *New Orleans Tribune,* January 2000, www.writers.net/writers/books/22907 (accessed October 7, 2005).

Italy Demands Retribution—1891

"New Orleans, 1891." www.americanlynching.com/infamous-old.html (accessed August 10, 2005).

Pontchartrain, Blake. "New Orleans Know-It-All" *Gambit Weekly,* www.bestofneworleans.com/dispatch/2006-04-25/blake.php (accessed September 11, 2004).

"Who Killa da Chief?" Court TV. www.crimelibrary.com/gangsters_outlaws/family_epics/marcello/3.html. (accessed August 10, 2005).

The Fight of the Century—1892

Fields, Armond. *James J. Corbett: A Biography of the Heavyweight Boxing Champion and Popular Theater Headliner.* Jefferson, N.C.: McFarland & Co., 2001.

Haley, Melissa. "Storm of Blows." *Common-Place,* January 2003, www.historycooperative.org/journals/cp/vol-03/no-02/haley/haley-2.shtml (accessed October 18, 2004).

Hickok, Ralph. "Jim Corbett." www.hickoksports.com/biograph/corbettj.shtml (accessed October 19, 2004).

International Boxing Hall of Fame."Corbett was King of a New Era." Legends and Lore, www.ibhof.com/ibhfhvy2.htm (accessed October 18, 2004).

"Two Big Fighters Meet." *The New York Sun,* November 10, 1887.

The Silver Screen Finds a Home—1896

"American Vitagraph Company known as Vitagraph." Learn About Movie Posters, http://www.learnaboutmovieposters.com/NewSite/History/STUDIOS/Early%20Studios/VITAGRAPH/vitagraph.asp (accessed November 2, 2005).

Keith, Don Lee. "The first picture show: One hundred years ago this month, the first movie theater in the nation opened, right here in New Orleans." *New Orleans Magazine,* July 1996.

Rossell, Deac. "William T. ('Pop') Rock, American exhibitor, executive." *Who's Who of Victorian Cinema,* www.victorian-cinema.net/rock.htm (accessed October 4, 2005).

Stall, Buddy. "First movie theater in the U.S." *The Clarion Herald,* March 16, 2000.

Working for the Vote—1903

"Chapter III: The National American Convention of 1903" In *History of Woman Suffrage,* vol. 5: 1900–1920. New York: National American Woman Suffrage Association, 1922.

National American Woman Suffrage Association Collection Home Page. lcweb2.loc.gov/ammem/naw/nawsa.html (accessed November 14, 2004).

Shaw, Anna. "The Story of a Pioneer." http://www.electricscotland.com/history/america/pioneerndx.htm (accessed November 19, 2004).

Like a Bird in the Sky—1910

"Early Aviation in Louisiana: The 1910 New Orleans Aviation Tournament." lsm.crt.state.la.us/aviation/aviation.htm (accessed August 4, 2005)

"Early Birds of Aviation." www.earlyaviators.com/index.htm (accessed August 4, 2005).

Striegel, Lawrence. "The Greatest Show Above Earth." *Newsday,* www.newsday.com/community/guide/lihistory/ny-past1031,0,6229656.story?coll=ny-lihistory (accessed August 8, 2005).

Villard, Henry Serrano. *The Story of the Early Birds.* New York: Thomas Y. Crowell Company, 1968.

Dynamiting Helps Save the City—1927

Barry, John. *Rising Tide.* New York: Simon and Schuster, 1997.

"Louisiana Timeline." *Encyclopedia Louisiana.* www.enlou.com/time/year1927.htm (accessed November 8, 2005).

"Raging Rivers Wild: A Look at the Flood of 1927." *Ashley County Ledger.* http://www.ashleycountyledger.com/articles/2003/10/18/history/z999.txt (accessed August 9, 2005).

Building the Boat that Won the War—1944

Higgins Industries. www.google.com/search?q=cache:O6AepzAlw94J:www.higginsboat.org/html/higind.html+higgins+pt+boats+new+orleans&hl=en&gl=us&ct=clnk&cd=3 (accessed August 4, 2005).

Jefferson, William J. "Reintroduction of the Higgins Gold Medal Resolution." *The Jefferson Report,* June 6, 2001.

Torbett, Melanie. "Built for War." Higgins LCVP (New Orleans D-Day Museum), www.acbs-bslol.com/Porthole/HigginsLCVP.htm (accessed August 4, 2005).

Widmer, Mary Lou. "Making of the A-Bomb at Higgins Industries in New Orleans." www.crt.state.la.us/crt/tourism/lawwii/Higgins/Higgins_ABomb.htm (accessed August 4, 2005).

At the End of a Streetcar Line—1946

Fargo, Emily Lane. "Theater-by-the-Grove presents A Streetcar Named Desire." Historical Background, www.turgingsome drama.com/streetcar/streetcarbackground.htm (accessed November 13, 2005).

Gussow, Mel. "Hey, Stell-Lahhh! Where's That Rattletrap Streetcar?" *New York Times,* May 1, 2001, Arts section.

Nelson, Davia and Nikki Silva. "Lost and Found Sound." National Public Radio, May 28, 1999.

"Tennessee Williams' New Orleans." The Denver Center for the Performing Arts, www.denvercenter.org/pdf/111.pdf (accessed November 5, 2005).

Another Day at School—1960

Bridges, Ruby. *Through My Eyes.* New York: Scholastic, 1999.

Coles, Robert. *The Story of Ruby Bridges.* New York: Scholastic, 1995.

Hunter-Gault, Charlayne. "A Conversation with Ruby Bridges Hall, February 18, 1997: A Class of One." www.pbs.org, Search: "Ruby Bridges" (accessed August 11, 2005).

Burying the Musician—2004

Coclanis, Angelo P., and Peter A. Coclanis. "Jazz funeral: a living tradition." *Southern Cultures,* Summer 2005, vol. 11, 86.

Donze, Frank. "Tuneful Tomb. The *Times-Picayune*, October 24, 2004, http://64.233.187.104/search?q=cache:_ue2vlpUt6MJ:nolalive.com/news/t-p/index.ssf%3F/base/news-5/1098600920155541.xml+%22lloyd+Washington%22+%22new+Orleans%22+tomb+Donze&hl=en (accessed August 16, 2005).

Hart, Lianne. "Unsung musicians honored with final place to rest. *Los Angeles Times,* September 12, 2004, www.boston.com/news/nation/articles/2004/09/12/unsung_musicians_honored_with_final_place_to_rest/ (accessed August 16, 2005).

LeGardeur, Lili. "Grand Finale." *Gambit Weekly.* www.bestofneworleans.com/dispatch/2004-08-03/news_feat.html (accessed June 3, 2005).

And the Water Rushed through the City—2005

"Hurricane Katrina Makes Landfall." WTOL 11, Toledo's *News Leader,* August 29, 2005.

"Scenes from a broken city." The *Times-Picayune,* August 29, 2005, www.nola.com/weblogs/print.ssf?/mtlogs/nola_Times-Picayune/archives/print074983.html (accessed December 11, 2005).

"Storm That Drowned a City." *NOVA,* www.pbs.org/wgbh/nova/orleans/how-flash.html (accessed December 12, 2005).

INDEX

ABOUT THE AUTHOR

Bonnye E. Stuart is a ninth-generation New Orleanian and member of the Perret family. She grew up in the city amid thirty-nine first cousins and lots of aunts and uncles. Her four children were all born in New Orleans. She got her bachelor's in advertising from the Manship School of Journalism at Louisiana State University and received her master's in communication from the University of New Orleans. She writes short stories, poems, and plays, many of which are based on her life in New Orleans. She presently teaches at Winthrop University in South Carolina.